D1570261

STREET CORNER CONSERVATIVE

He found himself filled with a supernatural courage that came from nowhere . . . he did not think of himself as the representative of the corps of gentlemen . . . But he did feel himself as the ambassador of all these common and kindly people in the street . . .

G. K. Chesterton
The Man Who Was Thursday

STREET CORNER CONSERVATIVE

WILLIAM F. GAVIN

ARLINGTON HOUSE · PUBLISHERS
NEW ROCHELLE, NEW YORK

The following copyrighted material is reprinted with the permission of the publishers:

The "Tivoli Theatre" episode in Chapter 1 reprinted with permission from the April 22, 1964 edition of the *Jersey Journal*, Jersey City, N.J.

Material from "A Conservatives Liberal Education," Chapter 3 reprinted with permission from the *Alternative* magazine, Bloomington, Ind. edition of December 1971 and from *National Review* magazine, N.Y., N.Y. edition of December 3, 1971.

Material from "Looking for the Invisible Man," Chapter 4 reprinted with permission from *Human Events*, Washington D.C. edition of September 8, 1973.

Material from the "Reaction" section of Chapter 5 reprinted with permission from *National Review* magazine, N.Y., N.Y. edition of December 3, 1971.

Library of Congress Catalog Card Number ______________

ISBN 0-87000-325-9 __________

Library of Congress Cataloging in Publication Data

Gavin, William F
Street corner conservative.

Includes index.
1. Conservatism--United States. I. Title.
JA84.U5G33 320.5'2'0973 75-11710
ISBN 0-87000-325-9

Manufactured in the United States of America

This book is dedicated

to my father

1907-1942

". . . his tears burned my cheeks and
his heart moved in mine . . ."

Dylan Thomas,
Poem in October

Contents

Foreword

In the spring of 1971 I traveled to South Vietnam as an officer of the United States Information Agency. When I arrived in Saigon, I met another USIA officer who had previously served in Vietnam and who was now part of the same orientation tour. I asked him if he had any advice that might help me understand the Vietnamese.

"There are two things you have to know about the Vietnamese," he said. "The first thing is that they are not at all like us. The second is that they are very much like us. Once you understand this, everything else will fall into line."

It was the most sensible advice I received from anyone concerning the Vietnamese. They are, indeed, different from Americans, different in outlook and history and habit and custom. But they are also very much like us. The alleged Vietnamese inherent tendency to corruption is no more inherent than the alleged tendency toward corruption of certain New Jersey politicians. The Vietnamese want a good life for their children. They want to be prosperous and at peace. They want justice. In basic things they are very, very much like us.

The urban and street corner conservatives I write of are differferent from other Americans—in ways which I hope this book will make clear—but they are, at the same time, also like other Americans. They do not want to overthrow the system. But they are not quite satisfied with the system either. They supported the United States efforts in Vietnam, but at the same time deplored the strategy of piecemeal escalation which led to such a disastrous state of affairs. They are sick unto death with the follies and the arrogance of liberal Democrats, but they have not quite snuggled up to the Republican party. They are, to quote Norman Mailer quoting André Gide, not to be understood too quickly—which, I fear, is precisely what has been happening to them.

It seems in recent years that not a month has passed without someone publishing an article or a book about "blue-collar" or "ethnic" Americans or whatever label is used to describe Americans who share, basically, the same socially and morally conservative view of the world but who are not usually thought of as conservatives. I have read most of these and I am never quite certain just what the authors have in mind. Some see the urban conservatives as merely a new kind of black American, i.e., someone about whom liberal intellectuals can write compassionate articles and books, with the emphasis heavy on injustice and the need for federal programs to rectify the injustice. Others see some political gain to be made by rediscovering urban conservatives. These discoveries have, for the most part, been made by moderate liberal intellectuals of the Democratic party. Their new-found sympathy for the working class urban conservative has always seemed suspect to me.[1] Where were these intellectuals when the urban conservatives really needed them in the nineteen-sixties? They were formulating or propagandizing for programs whose ultimate effect, unintentional perhaps but deadly, was to stick it to the urban conservatives. As an old Jersey City boy I always get suspicious when people who have been ignoring me or kicking me around suddenly start to treat me sweetly.

1. The exception to this is the excellent work of Father Andrew Greeley. His books about the Irish in America, *That Most Distressful Nation*, and the ethnics, *Why Can't They Be Like Us?* are invaluable. I disagree with some of his political views, but find him the very best of the liberal writers on the topics covered in this book.

While it would be presumptuous of me to say that I am "the" or even "a" voice of urban conservatism, I recognize that voice when I hear it, especially when it comes out of my own mouth. Unlike the liberals who only now are admitting the follies of liberalism, trying desperately to get back into the good graces of urban conservatives, I have remained, philosophically, just about where I was—with modifications in style and, I hope, depth—in Jersey City twenty years ago. This is not, therefore, a book by a reformed liberal intellectual or any kind of intellectual (a fact that will become clear after the first few pages if it is not so already), but a book about urban conservatives by someone who, in the most important ways, is very much like them and always has been.

There are three words or phrases I use throughout the book that need a word of explanation. I use "philosophy" in the sense of "guidance in practical affairs" and not in the sense of some systematic explanation of the universe. "Urban conservative" refers to those who are conservative but who have not, for various reasons, reflected on their conservatism. For the most part they do live in the cities, but I want to stress here the fact that many of them have moved, often following the lead of their grown children, to the suburbs. "Urban conservative" is not, therefore, limited by geography but by outlook. A man living in Lyndhurst, New Jersey, for three years after having spent a lifetime in Jersey City is, by my definition, still an "urban conservative," even if his conservatism is unarticulated, unexamined and visceral.

What about "street corner conservative?" By this I mean anyone who has been raised in the kind of urban, usually Catholic, background I describe, and who is conscious of his conservatism and able intellectually to defend its premises. One draft of the book used "street corner conservative" to refer to both groups, the "gut" and the "knowing" conservative, but things started to get confusing. Thus the two terms; quite arbitrary, but my own.

I want to acknowledge the help and advice of Richard Whalen, Dick Wheeler and Jameson Campaigne, all of whom showed faith in the project. Needless to say, I am solely and totally responsible for the opinions, conclusions, analyses, and faults of this book. I point out this obvious fact only because I am now employed by Senator James L. Buckley for whom I have boundless admiration as a Senator and as a human being. I want to make it clear I wrote this book not as Senator Buckley's assistant but on my own as an American exercising freedom of speech. The anticipated brickbats and the bouquets (if any) should be directed to me.

My sincere thanks to the publishers of the *Jersey Journal, Human Events,* the *Alternative,* and *National Review* for giving me permission to use material written by this author and previously published by them.

What I have attempted to do is write about the kind of world in which I grew up and in which I was educated and came to manhood. I believe that world represents a different kind of American conservatism, which I call "street corner conservatism," and that this kind of conservatism will become increasingly important in American political and social life.

I hope this book will tell you an important fact about us: we are not at all like you and we are very much like you.

Chapter 1
A Jersey City Education

> One has only to read Machiavelli's history of Florence to see that living in a beautiful city is not in itself enough to bring out the best in one. So far as their humanity is concerned, the people of, say, Jersey City, compare very favorably to the Florentines of the era of that city's greatest glory . . .
>
> —Edward Banfield, *The Unheavenly City*

For years I have had a fantasy. I sit in a chair at the head of a long conference table. Around the table are the publishers and editors of the top newspapers and magazines, the heads of the networks and all of the prestigious liberal columnists. (It is a rather large table, admittedly, but this is my fantasy.) I rise and say:

"Gentlemen, you are probably wondering why I called you here. I want to let you in on a little secret. You have been

writing about people you call "ethnics" or "blue-collars" or whatever label is now fashionable and your television programs have been devoting some news time to them. But, gentlemen, you don't know what the hell you are talking about. Listen to what I am going to say, gentlemen, because I am only going to say it once. You may take notes. Do you really want to know what it is like to be the kind of person you have ignored for so many years and now are trying to placate with silly, misinformed, êlitist-based nonsense? This is how it was for one street corner conservative. It is not typical. But it is true and perhaps you can learn from it. It goes like this:

Jersey City . . .

Trying to describe the place where you grew up is like trying to describe your own face. You take so much of it for granted. By the time you do learn to stand aside and examine familiar things for their strangeness, you no longer can *feel* the place the way you did when you were living there day-by-day.

But the attempt must be made, for my conservatism is rooted, so to speak, in concrete. It is a conservatism of city neighborhoods. Growing up in a neighborhood may be different now. I've been away from my old neighborhood for a long time and really don't have much to do with city life except to ride through the city or work in it. Yet, for many years the neighborhood wasn't a place to pass through—it was the entire universe for me. When my father died my mother and I moved from the Greenville section to Van Horne Street in the Lafayette section, to the brick, six-family, three-story building across the street from Our Lady of Assumption Church. My mother had lived as a young girl in the very same rooms but at the time, in August of 1942, only my grandmother lived there. My Uncle John, a bachelor who lived with her, had at age forty-two been drafted into the Army.

I came to know Lafayette through names—Dolski and Malinoski and Gulairdi and Whritenour and Mikolajczyk. And places—Lafayette Park, known only as "the park," the Jersey City Printing Company, All Saints Church, Westinghouse Elevator Corporation, Ames Steel Works, the Tivoli movie theater, the area on Communipaw Avenue where my mother and her girl friends had played. And legends—how the family had run out of the rooms on Halliday Street the night of the Black Tom explosion in 1917. There was a character to Lafayette that has been lacking in every other place I have ever lived. This does not mean I harbor some kind of romantic desire to return to Lafayette. I have changed and the world has changed and Lafayette has changed and, in all concerns that really matter, I can't go to that home again.

But, back then, when someone asked you where you came from, you said, "Lafayette" (pronounced Laff-ee-ett') and expected everyone to know what that meant, the subtleties and nuances of that neighborhood compared with Greenville (a lot of two-family houses), Downtown ("tough" but close to Lafayette in spirit), Marion (Italian), Hudson City (for reasons never quite clear to me, not quite part of Jersey City in spirit, more like a regular city) and, of course, the area around the Hudson County Boulevard and Journal Square: "Rich," almost official in nature, a place one passed through or where one attended a first-run movie, not at all like Lafayette.

An example of the difficulty in explaining Lafayette: years after we moved from Lafayette I joined the Army and as part of my training, spent eight weeks in Valley Forge, Pennsylvania, General Hospital as a medical technician trainee. One weekend I went to Philadelphia (for the first time in my life although it is only ninety miles away from Jersey City; provincialism and a baseball knowledge that Philadelphia was known for the awful Phillies had worked together to keep me out of Philadelphia). I went with some other young soldiers and we saw a movie, Vittorio De Sica's *Umberto D*, a brilliant and neglected film in the neo-realistic style. On the way back we passed through the heart of North Philadelphia. One of the soldiers who had grown up in the suburbs of Connecticut looked at the rows of flats and said:

"Look at this, these are regular slums."

I was shocked because I had just been about to say that the neighborhood reminded me of Lafayette. Slums are dirty places where people throw garbage out the windows and where there's dope and gangs. Lafayette was not at all like that. But for the first time in my life I came across that almost total lack of familiarity with urban living that characterizes so many Americans. My Lafayette was not a slum. I say this not in any defensive way but merely as a matter of fact. In order to understand the people of Lafayette and the kind of people they represent you have to understand that the way they lived their lives, the kind of people they were—and are—makes it impossible for them to live in a slum. This may sound self-serving, but it is a matter of fact and must be understood as such.

My Lafayette-universe was inhabited by two kinds of people: family and friends. There were other kinds of people, but they played character parts or served as background players in the main dramas of our lives. For all I knew about the people who lived in the houses down near the "farms," the coal-dust-grit-encrusted lots where we played baseball; they could have been living in Tierra del Fuego. I walked past the ramshackle two- and three-storey wooden buildings on Woodward Street every day in the summer, but as far as I was concerned the only purpose they served was to limit any long hit someone might make in a baseball game.

The proximity of people in a neighborhood doesn't always mean their closeness in spirit or interest. Growing up in Lafayette meant living in a world within a number of worlds, a world in which you moved with almost uncanny precision without getting mixed up, except peripherally, in other worlds. Diagonally across the street from 232 Van Horne Street were two 4-storey flats, on each floor of which were Negro families ("black" was not yet fashionable). Aside from two names—Jesse and Angelina—I can't recall a single detail about the black people who lived there. I almost never played with them. I rarely talked to them and they rarely came to our end of the block to play.

Anyone who has not known a neighborhood may see this as a confession of urban racism. But that is untrue. It was simply another part of that kind of life-style, combining a sense of real community (no matter what color you were or what your name was, Lafayette was part of you) and individual and family freedom. Nobody bothered you and you didn't bother anybody. It may not be sociologically sound, but it worked.[2]

What made Lafayette a community? A difficult, probably unanswerable, question for no one was quite certain just where Lafayette began or ended. To most Jersey City people it was the place you ride through on the Greenville bus in order to get downtown from Greenville. But I think it is safe to say that what made Lafayette unique is an attitude, one which I absorbed over the years I spent there as a boy, and one which I still find coloring so much of what I do as a man.

Skepticism is not quite the word, and cynicism is too strong, but there was a certain sense of "you-can't-fool-me" and "I'm no sucker" about almost everyone in Lafayette. Standing on the corner of Woodward Street and Communipaw Avenue I would listen to the big guys talk. They were never "serious." To be serious was to be . . . well, to be serious—and seriousness itself—just wasn't accepted. "Kidding" was the thing. If you could "kid," if you could show that no matter how foolish anyone else was to believe x or y or z, *you* weren't being fooled—then you were a true Lafayette boy.[3]

Now this does not mean that those who wise-cracked were as cynical or as shrewd as they seemed. What we aimed for was an air of knowing-it-all . . . and how little any of us knew! We were city boys and city men and we were as innocent of the great world as if we had lived our lives in monasteries. Of all the people in the world, those who grew up in the Jersey City of Frank Hague and John V. Kenny were anything but truly cynical. We believed, how we believed! But we never admitted we believed and our defiance, our instinct to refuse to show anything approaching sentimentality, gave everyone in Lafay-

2. On the other hand, the unquestioned intellectual élite in Lafayette were the Madison family—and they were Negroes. Tommy Madison taught me Latin when I was learning to be an altar boy. His mother, Dr. Lena Edwards, was years later awarded the Medal of Freedom by President Johnson, for work among the poor.

3. Father Andrew Greeley, in *That Most Distressful Nation* (Chapter 5), discusses the role of ridicule among the Irish. Until I read his analysis, I had thought "kidding around" was an exclusively Lafayette-Jersey City phenomenon.

ette the kind of attitude best exemplified by James Cagney's roles in his great, tough-guy movies for Warner Brothers. Jaunty, devil-may-care, "Whatya say, whatya know," chew gum, jingle-jangle change in your pockets, get dressed up on Saturday night and look for girls. On Sunday afternoons, after Mass, the corner of Woodward and Communipaw looked like a James Cagney film festival.

At the time, of course, I had no way of knowing that there were other ways of looking at the world. Protestant, nice, middle-America ways; sharp-funny Jewish urban ways which were quite similar to those of Lafayette—I never knew people looked at the world any differently.

Even today, I find myself, knowing what I am doing as I am doing it but unable to stop, sliding into the Jimmy Cagney, smile-while-you're-hurt, don't-let-them-know-you-care attitude. Maybe that was it. No one wanted himself to know that he cared and no one wanted anyone else to know that he cared.

Cared about what? About anything. Girls? Don't let anyone know you like that girl or else they'll tease you. Sports? Don't let anyone know you want to make the team because if you don't, they'll be on you. Ambition? You have none except to get some money and buy a car because doing that shows you know the "real" world. Teamwork? Only if you play a high school sport or if you are on a neighborhood team—but don't *talk* about it—just do it.

Yet Lafayette cannot be defined in one attitude. There were a dozen worlds within 20 or 30 city blocks. On Van Horne Street we played houseball by standing close to the building, throwing the pink rubber ball up to a ledge off which it would bounce, and then running to first base in the middle of the street, to our right. But on Woodward Street, only a block away, they ran to their *left*. Unheard of! Heretical! When there were inter-block games there would be heated arguments over which direction it was correct to run after you had hit the ball against the house.

Touch football? On Van Horne Street, the rules said, "Tagging in the backfield but no blocking the rusher." On Woodward Street, there was no tagging in the backfield but blocking the rusher was permitted. No arguments over theological quiddities ever generated so much heat and so little light as the arguments concerning the right way to play touch football, even if the "football" itself was a tightly, expertly rolled newspaper tied with cord. God only knows what sports perversions were allowed on Lafayette Street where no one from Woodward Street or Van Horne Street would ever dream of playing ball.

If you were of Slovak ancestry you attended Our Lady of Assumption School. If you were anything except Slovak, but still Catholic, you attended All Saints. I lived directly across the street from Assumption School and Church but never attended either, walking the six blocks to All Saints. Yet, All Saints was, to use the phrase now so popular, my "neighborhood" school in a way Assumption or Public School Number 22, a block away, never could be. Neighborhood was a concept more than a place. All of the spiritual and social and psychological history of my family was focused upon All Saints Church and its school, just as children of Slovak heritage thought nothing of walking ten or twelve blocks to Assumption, even if it meant walking past school 22 on the way. The important thing is that we chose to make that walk and that we chose to go to that school.

When we weren't going to school or playing boxball or houseball we were standing on a street corner or "hanging around." This is an urban art that defies both analysis and description. It is, in essence, the art of standing, slouching, crouching, or aimlessly walking about on a street corner. To the untutored eye it might seem like a way of wasting time, but to the person hanging out it is a revered custom, a social necessity and a way of life.

Although small children may, from time to time, stand on the same street corner as those who are hanging out, the children are not considered, even by themselves, to be hanging out until they reach high school age. There is a kind of chain-of-hanging-out life in most neighborhoods. Sixteen-year-olds begin to hang out as a minority. When they reach their late teens and early twenties, the golden age of hanging-out, they become the street corner majority. Then, when they marry they still hang out, but less frequently, and with less claim to street corner dominance. The last gasp of the young married man, so far as hanging-out is concerned, is Sunday afternoon when he will stand, very often with a majority of his own age group, until it's time to go watch the football game or have a few beers.

To someone not born and raised in a city, hanging-out invariably brings up one question: What do you *do* when you hang out? For one thing, you stand in one place, more or less, for over an hour and probably less than four hours. If you are alone, you lean against the building, with one leg propped up against the wall and watch cars go by. You wait for your friends to come along. If they don't come along, you stand there or move around the corner. If someone finally arrives to stand with you, you may or may not make conversation. The point is not to meet anyone, although if no one is there you spend your time waiting, but to be there with somebody. Once that is achieved, hanging-out develops naturally and the night might end with a whole cornerful of young men just standing there, not saying much, just being there, looking at the cars or girls pass by.

Hanging-out is the essence of neighborhood life. I have often thought that one of the difficulties keeping many urban conservatives out of the Republican party was that it is all but impossible to communicate with, say, a mid-western Protestant Republican who is a hard-line free-enterpriser if you have spent quite a bit of time in an activity his upbringing condemns as useless at best and probably sinful in its toleration of "doing nothing." How can you explain that hanging-out, although it may appear to be "doing nothing," is an important social custom in the city and that many important events transpire on street corners that ordinarily would not happen at all if people were expected to be "doing something" all the time?

We were all, I am convinced, conservatives. We never intellectually knew that we were, but instinctively, it seems, we knew that certain people and institutions and places have claims upon our loyalties. I believe that much of the furor that has accompanied the busing battle during the past few years might have been avoided if Supreme Court Justices had been given a seminar in Neighborhood Realities. It is inconceivable to me that intelligent men and women can so misunderstand, or worse, understand and ignore, the way most people feel about the neighborhood in which they live. Most city people have certain patterns of life built around a school or a church or a certain group of stores and anything that upsets that pattern is fiercely combatted. The revolt of the working class and middle-class families against forced busing for racial balance is a predictable result of neighborhood pride and could possibly have been avoided if neighborhoods had been understood for what they really are—not geographic entities—but spiritual and social realities to be tampered with only at great risk and peril.

And that was my Lafayette. Street corner wisecracks, Jimmy Cagney-toughness and resiliency were its virtues. The neighborhood was its universe and at the center of the universe was the family. For me that meant, for a few years, my mother and Grandma and the rest of the Cummings family. At 232 Van Horne Street my grandmother and my mother loved me and took care of me and worried about me. They had time for me. They made sure I got to school and was dressed warmly in winter. My God, how I have been loved! And that love is real to me, as real as the concrete sidewalks and the gray slate steps of 232 Van Horne and, in a very large sense, it is intertwined with all of the neighborhood life in my memory. How many young Americans in our time have been able to say similar things about their childhood, even (especially?) "privileged" suburban-raised kids of the generation after mine?

I have often wondered if it would not be useful to have a question included on police forms: Has the suspect been loved by parents or family? I wonder how often the answer would be no. Volumes have been written about urban ills and I have read quite a few books and articles—but in none can I find an examination of the relationship between loving families and social stability. I am too Roman Catholic (original sin and all that) and too Irish (moods, bitterness, rages) to suggest that family love can cure all social ills, but I feel there is a connection between city peace and family love that deserves sociological study.

My father's death is the first family event I can remember. Before that, there are flashes of memories: Uncle Benny, the short, dapper, lively railroad man standing on the sand at Manasquan Beach, throwing back his head, laughing at some joke; birthday parties in my cousin's home, complete with party hats; sitting in the grandstand with Uncle John at Roosevelt Stadium watching the Jersey Giants play . . . but my father's funeral is something different. The whole family, the Gavins and the Cummings, are there together.

I can see them in the hushed, flower-bedecked room at Larry Quinn's funeral home. My mother's brothers and sisters . . . even their plain, everyday names are part of my heritage. Now, my children grow up in a world where people are named Kim or Alison or Stacy or Dirk or Valerie. I grew up with people named Mary (Mamie) and Margaret ("Bar"), Helen, Grace, Ann (my mother) and Johnnie, Dick, and Jimmy. My father's funeral home wake forever banished to memory the funeral-in-the-parlor for the Cummings and Gavin families. But the sorrow, public and laced with ritual, the long hours of sitting in a room at the head of which is the embalmed, cosmetic-painted body of a loved one, his hands folded with a Rosary intertwined in his fingers . . . the first murmurs of conversation as those who have paid their respects see friends and even relatives they haven't seen in a long time, then slowly without anyone being aware of it the talk becomes louder and louder still, even the closest relatives of the deceased joining in, that in a while the room is filled with talk, talk that, for a few moments, takes them all away from the reason they are here . . . all of this remains. The food and drink for the mourners take on another form, becomes a meal in a restaurant for those who have attended the burial in Holy Name Cemetery.

The priest reads the Latin, comforting because the words of grief and loss are at once familiar and unknown as we stand around the graveside . . . flowers again . . . the drivers of the limousine holding their black peaked hats in their hands . . . the end of the prayers. A shriek, sobbing, someone—Uncle Dick?—puts his arm around my shoulder. We walk away from the grave.

Uncle Dick's wife, my Aunt Pauline, has been taking care of me during the few days of the arrangements for the wake and burial. She takes me to see "Bambi" at a movie theater at Journal Square, the business and entertainment center of Jersey City, a wide, multi-laned section of the Hudson County Boulevard (twenty-one years later it would be called John F. Kennedy Boulevard) with the enormous Stanley Theater (Warner Brother's pictures . . . Paramount Pictures . . . Bing Crosby . . . Errol Flynn) at the north, the Loew's Theater (MGM . . . Clark Gable . . . Mickey Rooney) on the west, the Hudson Tubes to 33rd Street in New York at the east and Bergen Avenue to the south, a block away from the State Theater (20th Century-Fox . . . Tyrone Power . . . Betty Grable) and along Sip Avenue near Bergen, the offices of the *Jersey Journal* and the Public Service Gas and Electric (for which I will someday read gas and electric meters while I attend Jersey City State College) and banks and lawyers' offices and insurance firms. Journal Square is part of the memory of this family event.

But most important of all is the Family. There is a kind of imbalance here. My mother's side of the family is much more familiar to me since I visit, quite often, with my cousins on that side of the family. The Cummings family begins and ends and has its life in one indomitable, strong, loving (but capable of quick Irish sharpness of tongue) person: Grandma.

Today, when Grandmas are so often prettier and shapelier than their daughters, my Grandmother becomes, in retrospect, almost a mythical figure. Small, with long, jet-black hair that she wore in a bun, her hair black even until she was in her seventies, with the ability to stare down even the oldest of her children and to reduce to jelly any of her grandchildren with what the family came to know as "sharp eyes"—Grandma was the living, beating heart of the Cummings family.

She was born, Margaret Morris, in the Hudson City section of the city when people still kept cows and chickens there. When she was a small girl her mother died, her father remarried and the family—now including stepsisters—moved to Cornelison Avenue. The landlord of the building into which they moved was named Cummings. My grandmother, Margaret Morris, married his son, William Cummings.

They had nine children. There were good times. There were

bad times. There was love and there was anger. Always, everywhere, there was the day-by-day struggle to raise a family in decency and pride. It wasn't easy.

Grandma survived all that. She survived by working in a factory during the first World War when Johnnie, only seventeen, had enlisted in the Army and Jimmy and Mamie were already married. She had small children to take care of and she worked back-breaking hours to do it. They were what is known as tough times. Indeed, in my family, unlike many other American families, tough times do not mean the depression years but the years immediately preceding and during World War I.

The family gradually became a group of men and women looking always toward Lafayette and "Mama," no matter where they went to live or who they married. Johnnie, a bachelor, remained with Grandma until she died. William ("Peewee") died young, his heart ruined by rheumatic fever, just before the death of my father. Jimmy married a girl from the neighborhood, had children, saw her die and then remarried. Dick married a previously married woman with a son. Helen married a neighborhood boy who worked as a janitor in the city schools and who in later years became head of a union of school employees.

Margaret married a man who would become a city detective . . . Grace married a mail clerk . . . years before, Mamie had married Benny, a jovial, happy-go-lucky railroader . . . and my mother married Bill Gavin from Saint Bridget's parish, a young, handsome, easy-going guy who worked in a box factory and later as a truckdriver.

There is a kind of urban poetry in their occupations: railroader, truckdriver, detective, mailman, janitor (Grandpa Gavin was a street cleaner). My relatives are the living flesh of the city, close to its streets and its people, unaware of, and uninterested in, sociological explanations for its ills or its wonders, totally un-self-conscious, absorbed only in the private griefs and joys of the life of the family. The Roman Catholic church and the Democratic party are the two major, unquestioned, foundations upon which their world is built.

They are all at the wake and the funeral. It is August and

their heavy blue suits and starched white collars and ties make the men sweaty and uncomfortable, but this is prior to the Age of Comfort in America and the Age of Rebellion is not within their chronologic or spiritual history. So they sit there, wilting in the heat, because it is also before the age of universal central air conditioning as an accepted—demanded—fixture of life and the ritual of death.

Johnnie is in the Army. It is his second war, in neither of which he saw action, but to both of which he went when, with the slightest pull by the boys down at the Hall, he could have stayed home. But it is not in his nature to ask for favors. He is a Cummings and a Morris combined: proud, stubborn, moody, *deep*. So it is decided it will be best for my mother and me to live with Grandmother.

And so we did. In September, 1942, I entered the third grade of All Saints Grammar School, with Sister Leo Maria, old and gentle and slightly forgetful, as my teacher.

School

Q. *Who made the world?*
A. *God made the world.*
Q. *Who is God?*
A. *God is the creator of heaven and earth and all things.*
Q. *Why did God make you?*
A. *God made me to know Him and love Him and serve Him in this world and to be happy with Him forever in the next.*

That—so far as memory serves—is the beginning of the *Baltimore Catechism* that was the foundation stone of the educational edifice built by the Roman Catholic church in the Diocese of Newark when I was growing up in Jersey City. In its form it is representative of much of Catholic education in those days: It provided both the answers and the questions, it left little room for ambiguity and was rooted in the belief that this world was not the only one and that man is not the most important thing in the universe.

Q. *What is man?*
A. *Man is a creature composed of body and soul.*

It has become fashionable, almost obligatory, to criticize the system of education of which this dogmatic question and answer, learning-by-rote approach was such a basic part. My own children go to public school and attend Saturday school for religious instruction. Their religion texts do not contain, as far as I can tell, any dogmatic assertions whatsoever. I am told that this is good, because the implanting of dogmatic assertions in the young brain, say the educational theorists, does grievous damage. So much for Aquinas and Newman.

I wonder. I was a high-school teacher myself for six years and I know that there are few things less instructive than rote learning—but one of the things that is less instructive than rote learning is the idea that there isn't anything at all to "learn," only things to "discuss." I taught in a parish Saturday school for a year and was told by students that my course in Church History was the only one where they were expected to know facts. Previously, they had been asked only for their opinions. But they *knew* what their opinions were. What they wanted to know was the facts of their religion—but few teachers had bothered to tell them, so eager were the teachers to avoid any contamination by indoctrination, rote learning and other Catholic school horrors.

But the nineteen-forties and early fifties were not yet a time for "discussion" in Catholic schools and I spent my years at Sacred Heart Grammar School and, after my father's death, All Saints Grammar School and Saint Michael's High School, absorbing or avoiding, depending upon my adherence to scholarly discipline, quite a bit of rote learning in many subjects.

Yet, looking back, I do not regret the education I received in Catholic schools. In many ways it was a good education, and in some ways it surpassed the "quality" education I have managed to attain, through higher earning power, for my own children.

Today the much-derided catechetical instruction is now as extinct as the dodo bird in Catholic schools. There is a part of my mind that knows such question-and-answer rote learning is as deadly dull and as liable to be swept away the minute it isn't needed for test answers as its most vehement critics say it is. However, the critics forget one virtue of old-style Catholic education: It sought to educate. It took as "given" the fact that human reason could apprehend truths, even truths about the Creator of the universe and that a substratum of rock-hard fact must underlie any educational system. Thus, the rock-hard questions and answers of the catechism.

And is there a better way of going about it? Who or what, indeed, did make the world? The Roman Catholic church claims to know. Why be defensive about it? I suppose that if the question is asked at all nowadays there is call for a discussion period in which John and Mary and George will give their opinions as to how this whole thing got started. There will be "sharing" of views and at the end of the class period it will be decided to resume the discussion tomorrow and everyone's assignment will be to bring in some newspaper or magazine article about the creation of the world.

I am, of course, reducing to the absurd. But the fact remains: the question-and-answer system was not all that bad. For one thing the answers were at once ingeniously simple yet intellectually respectable. Take the answer to the question: "What is man?"—"Man is a creature composed of body and soul." How much more immediately satisfying and how much more intellectually profound in the long run is that answer compared with the kind of non-answer that, I believe, most children get, if indeed they get anything of the sort at all, in today's schools.

There is, of course, a considerable philosophical difference of opinion on whether or not man is a creature composed of body and soul. There has even been a great and on-going controversy in the Western world for hundreds of years about whether soul and body are separate entities or, indeed, if "soul" and "body" are not simply code words for what is, at bottom, an intellectual con game being played by the Church. These controversies I can understand. What I cannot understand is the reluctance on the part of modern Catholic educators to make unequivocal statements about the philosophical position of the Church on this and other matters.

As all of this suggests, at the beginning of my own education is the Roman Catholic church. Baptism, altar boys, First Holy Communion, weddings, funerals, Rosaries, Choir boys, Confession, Confirmation, abstaining from meat on Friday, Sunday Mass, First Friday observance, miraculous medals, scapulars, novenas with the heartfelt singing of "Mother Dearest, Mother Fairest," followed by benediction of the Most Blessed Sacrament, Latin, priests, retreats . . . they are all irrevocably combined in my mind and heart with algebra and history and literature and gym and recess and lunch and French I and II and chemistry and geometry. It is a kind of American education that is disappearing if it has not already disappeared. It is the kind of education most urban conservatives have received. It is exotic and mysterious to others, however.

How many Americans, for example, know what it is to buy a Chinese baby? The eighth grade students of Sister Regina Mary in All Saints School "bought" Chinese babies in an excess of fervor hitherto unknown in the Western world. Pinned to the wooden border of the blackboard, which was black, unlike the more scientifically correct but, somehow, *wrong* greenboard in most classes today, was a poster on which, with every ten dollars contributed, Sister would paste a picture of an angel, signifying one more Chinese baby (who, as I recall, were all allegedly abandoned by parents) saved for Christ. The money went to the Society for the Propagation of the Faith and then to missionaries working in China. I was in the eighth grade in 1948. In September, 1949, Mao proclaimed Communist rule over all China. I often wonder what happened to the infants who were the recipients of our pennies and nickels and dimes.

Until I was thirteen, all of my teachers had been nuns. Today, when many nuns are leaving the convents or transforming the convents into ideological battlegrounds, it is difficult to remember that there was a time when a nun, far from being a symbol of fierce revolutionary fervor, was a reminder of the inner peace which is the only kind of peace Christ ever promised anyone[4]—and that only at the price of giving up all to come follow Him.

4. The words in the Mass are "peace in our day"—how much more realistic and attainable than that which our politicians have promised us—"peace in our time." Peace in our day is directed toward the individual—peace in our time toward the entire world. The former is not only possible, but demonstrably so. The latter . . . ?

The nuns of my childhood were not, however, all the same. There were saintly nuns and funny nuns and there were, unfortunately, nuns who, in retrospect, were psychologically-disturbed to an alarming degree, full of petty cruelty and sadistic tendencies which now, I understand, are discovered by psychological testing before a girl becomes a nun. Most of the nuns were amazingly individualistic because of, rather than despite, their uniformity of dress and manner. They had no need to prove their femininity or their worth, so they were themselves and, as themselves, were on the whole unforgettable and on the whole delightful. I wonder how they look upon their orders today, when the younger members quote Dan Berrigan instead of the Holy Father?

The Church in recent years has fallen upon bad days. When I was young it was One, Holy, Catholic and Apostolic to its membership. But in recent years many of its members have brought forth an alphabetic litany of abuse. To them the Roman Catholic church is:

Authoritarian, bigoted, crass, dangerous (to civil liberties), embarrassing, fanatical, greedy, heartless, illiberal, jesuitical, know-nothing, legalistic, merciless, negative, outdated, paternalistic, quixotic, repressive, sadistic, totalitarian, unwise, vicious, waning, xenophobic (in America) and zestless.

That's what all the Best Minds in the Best Catholic periodicals have been saying. Enemies of the Church have been, of course, much more restrained in their criticism.

My education in All Saints School and Saint Michael's High School would not have gained the Good Education Seal of Approval. For one thing there was a tendency on the part of some of our nuns to equate Catholicism with Excellence in all fields.

If a human being was a Catholic, that was fine; if he was a poet, that was fine, too; but to be a Catholic poet was sublimity itself in their eyes. I have never met anyone who has ever heard of, let alone read, any poems by such Catholic verse luminaries as Helen Parry Eden, Katherine Tynan, Francis Carlin, Caroline Elizabeth MacGill, Edward F. Garesche, S.J., Francis J. Rock, S.S., and Sister Mary Bertrand, R.S.M.

But we memorized them and discussed them side-by-side with Keats and Shelley and Poe and the ever-popular William

Cullen Bryant. It has always been my secret hope that some scholar would begin a revival of, say, the works of Caroline Elizabeth MacGill or Helen Parry Eden or Francis J. Rock, S.S. But no such revival has occurred, so I am reduced to dropping their names quite casually into cocktail party conversation for my own amusement. No one dares to ask just who the hell they were for fear of being caught napping concerning some avant-garde poet.

Then, of course, there was that terrible Popish propaganda against which Paul Blanchard and other liberals warned Real Americans for years. Here, in its shameless entirety, is the cover story of the School Edition of *Our Little Messenger* for November 4, 1942:

ST. MARTIN AND THE BEGGAR

Brr! What a cold day it was!

The wind was sharp as a knife.

It cut into the very bones of the old beggar. "Help, help!" he cried.

Some Roman soldiers stopped.

"What do you want?" they asked.

The beggar held out his hands.

"Help me," he cried, "or I shall die. Will nobody help a poor man?"

"Ha!" laughed the soldiers.

"We are poor, too. But wait, here is Martin. Let us see whether he will help you."

Martin looked at the poor man.

"I wish I could help you," he said. "But all my money is gone."

"Ha, ha!" the soldiers laughed again. "Martin gives away his money."

Martin saw that the man was cold and sick. At once he took out his knife. He cut his soldier's cape into two parts. One part he gave to the beggar. The other part he kept for himself.

But what do you think happened that night? Martin woke up suddenly. He saw before him Our Lord with the beggar's part of the cape.

"Thank you, Martin," said Jesus.

Ah! Now Martin knew that the beggar was really our Lord. Martin became a great saint.

Next week you will read more about this great man of God.

No wonder liberal Americans have long deplored parochial schools. Think of it: A story in which a soldier, of all people, exercises charity to a poor man, not to "the poor," that all-purpose abstraction, but to a single, needy, individual human being, by giving the man half of what he needs most—in this case his cloak. No mention of the need for government aid. No plea on Martin's part to the authorities to help the poor man. He saw the shivering beggar and helped him, himself, just like that!

To the liberal mind, this concentration on personal moral responsibility, on the connection between acts of charity and the love of God is embarrassing. For years the liberals have been preaching the gospel according to Big Government. If a liberal had been writing for *Our Little Messenger*, it might have gone this way:

> Brr! What a cold day it was!
>
> The wind was sharp as a knife!
>
> It cut into the very bones of an old beggar. "Help, help!" he cried.
>
> The local war on Beggary volunteer asked the beggar to fill out a form. After that the beggar received on-the-job training and lived happily ever after.[5]

If I were asked to state the major differences between the kind of grammar school education I received and the kind my own children are receiving in the public schools of Arlington, Virginia, I wouldn't state it in terms of cost-per-pupil, class-size or equipment, although my children's schools get more money, have smaller classes and are loaded with wonderful gadgetry. I would, instead, quote from the message that appeared on the back of the report card that parents had to sign c. 1948 in All Saints School in Jersey City:

5. Milton Friedman put it this way: "I'm strongly in favor of charitable activities, whether individual or joint. One of the worst features of the current system of Social Security and welfare arrangements is that it has drastically reduced the feeling of obligation that members of society traditionally felt toward others. Children today feel far less obligation toward their parents than they did 50 years ago. If the state is going to take care of the parents, why should the children worry? Similarly with the poor. Who feels a personal obligation to help the poor? That's the Government's job now." Interview in *Playboy*, February, 1972.

TO PARENTS

The time after school up to supper should be given children for play. Sunlight and exercises at games will keep them healthy in soul and body.

Preparation of the next day's lessons should follow supper before the fatigue comes. Parents may help by hearing them recite but should give no special lessons as they have enough to do in meeting the requirements of their regular teacher.

Never permit them out of call after dark. Waywardness invariably starts with night street walking. Exact obedience in all things, and let parents be united in every correction, the one never petting when the other punishes.

Send them to school every day. Truant-playing in boys often begins with parents keeping them at home for some slight cause, and even girls lose interest in their classes when torn from their studies. See that they are on time, for it is but a step from the tardy scholar to the truant.

Be sure that they attend their religious duties on Sunday, and have a prayer book or beads. On Confession Day see that they go at the time appointed for them, and not at night, when they are in the way of grown people, besides contracting the habit of being out of doors after dark.

The Catholic School for which Priests, Religious teachers and people are sacrificing so much, can effect the good intended only with the co-operation of parents. As you value your own and your children's salvation and temporal happiness, join us in the great work of preserving to God and America this generation.

The authoritarian premises, the genteel, phraseology, the belief that one "contracts" the "habit" of staying out after dark, the obvious intrusion into the right of the parents to see to their children's upbringing according to their lights, and the final urging for co-operation in the name of God and America—how distant, in light years of style and content, from the modern report card. How strange, how very, very unlike everything we believe now.

Yet there is a kind of glory about the "To Parents" message. It reminds me that there was a time when I was part of a community—not only geographically, but spiritually—when there was not only a concern for grades but a concern for the entire moral life of the child entrusted to the care of "the

Catholic school for which Priests, Religious teachers and people are sacrificing" (note the descending order of importance), when it was the principal of the school and not the local television station who asked parents if they knew where their children were. I wonder if my own children are missing something once taken for granted which, although I didn't know it at the time, helped me to grow up in a decent and generally happy way.

We, Studs Lonigan's children, Bill Gavin-the-truckdriver's children are different now. We have gone to "secular" schools, a fate almost worse than excommunication, according to the nuns of my day, and have survived and even prospered. We are vigilant against intrusion into our lives whether it is from church or state. We would think no more of consulting the local pastor (busy himself, poor man, with coffeehouses and learning how to sing "The Sounds of Silence") about personal problems than we would the local police chief. We have gone out into the secular, non-Irish, non-Catholic world and, quite often, have been able to keep up with those who did not, as we did, look upon secular success as a possible form of spiritual failure from early childhood.

Our kids don't have teachers like One-Hail Mary Murphy, the priest who taught religion by throwing blackboard erasers at bold students and who was legendary for giving one Hail Mary as penance, no matter how odious or numerous the sins. (Hitler: "Bless me Father, I killed millions of innocent people." Murphy: "One Hail Mary, my boy!") Kids today have, instead, the best-trained, most highly-educated, best-paid teachers in America. They are going to succeed in ways we never would have dreamed of, we who went directly from high school to the blueprint room of the Westinghouse plant on Pacific Avenue because no one, absolutely no one in our family on either side, had ever gone to college.

But every now and then I look at my children and I think that when they get a bit older, I am going to tell them what Saint Bernard once said. He said: "If we see things more clearly and further off than our ancestors it is because we stand on the shoulders of giants." And I am going to tell them about the unknown giants—small giants to be sure, but giants on whose shoulders they stand—nuns they never knew, One-Hail Mary Murphy, Mr. Jones (not his real name), who taught "law" when he was sober, but who also taught us that a man could be intelligent and masculine at the same time. I'm going to tell them about those giants because they really should know.

Movies

When I was growing up—or whatever it is you do between the ages of 10 and 14—in Jersey City in the years after World War II, I spent a great deal of time in a neighborhood movie theatre, the Tivoli. Even now, years after the Tivoli showed its final film, I can, on Friday evenings, feel nostalgic and a bit sad. Friday evenings were the bright spot of the week for all of us, for it was then we reveled in the three-feature movies, numerous cartoons, the weekly chapter of the serial, newsreels, coming attractions and, in general, all around entertainment which, more often than not, included a fist fight or a small riot in the front rows.

We would emerge from this cinematic orgy, groggy and punch-drunk from the film feast and the sheer amount of time spent in absorbing all the images, satisfied that the week, despite such obvious nonsense as school and homework, was not a total loss.

Now the Tivoli, or the Tiv as it was known to its friends of whom I was one of the staunchest, was a huge, dirty, red-brick building, incredibly cold in winter and equipped with what can only be called primitive seating arrangements. In fact, one of the added attractions of the Tivoli, as opposed to the movie palaces at Journal Square, was the outside chance that you might see a seat or, if you were really fortunate, half a row of seats topple over if a patron didn't approach his seat with the proper amount of caution. In the summer, the Tiv, scorning such new-fangled devices as air-conditioning, attempted to placate its customers by blowing hot air into their faces from a machine which very well might have been a wind tunnel gone mad. Children were always warned of the danger of contracting a stiff neck or a cold in the joints or some other dread ailment, when planning to visit the Tiv during the summer.

Yet, the Tivoli was more than this. It was, strictly speaking, a way of life. It was murdered by television and, since I was one of those who, ever eager for new baubles, sold out to the then new, but now how conventional, how weary, joys of the "video," as it was called by one of our parish priests, I was an accessory to the murder. Admittedly, I did attend the last program ever shown at the Tivoli, but to my eternal shame I cannot now remember the names of the two films shown on that terrible night.

I can, however, remember my desperate, fervent hope that the Tiv would open again in a few weeks, that it had shut down only for repairs. But there was no reason to hope. The Tiv died that night and, despite a recurrent dream I had for almost a year afterward, it never again came to life. Its empty, mocking corpse, complete with that most definite sign of the death of a theatre—a marquee without words—stood for years on Communipaw Avenue, a monument to man's fickle heart and something we call progress.

I know I shall never feel about a place the way I felt about the Tivoli. It is trite to remark on the pure joys of childhood, the clear and heartfelt involvement of listening to a story well-told or, especially in my own generation, the gripping excitement of a thriller in the movies. But the Tivoli itself, for all its bad ventilation and dangerous furniture, was a joy.

On a typical Friday evening, we would congregate on the corner of Woodward Street and Communipaw Avenue and walk to the Tivoli, three long city blocks away. If we arrived before the doors opened, we would look in at the posters announcing coming attractions and make plans for the week ahead. Admission was 35 cents or, if you were younger or could convince the jaded ticket salesman you were younger than twelve, 11 cents. We always sat in the same section of the house, as did the groups (we weren't called "gangs" and "group" isn't exactly the word, but it is closer) from other sections of Lafayette.

When the lights went out—they never went down, they simply went out—a cheer welcomed the first movie which was always a cowboy film. Tex Ritter, Lash LaRue, Charles Starrett, William "Red Ryder" Elliott; all the class Z cowboy stars, fighting and singing their way through the same plot. Gabby Hayes and Al "Fuzzy" St. John usually played the role of the comic sidekick.

But the constant in all the films was an actor named Charles King who specialized in the role of a bully-boy, usually named "Lefty" or "Blacky." King, whose fierce moustache and glowering eyes graced hundreds of these films, usually was restricted in mood to a scowl or, when given a knowing nod from the bad-guy-in-chief, perhaps a sardonic grin. King became a favorite of the Tivoli audience, whose members acted perverse, perhaps, but were loyal in their choice of idols.

Charley King, where are you now, in this era of sick, mentally-disturbed badmen? You were bad for the pure joy of it, and if you wound up on the floor of the saloon, or in the dust of the street, rubbing your jaw, hatless, we knew that you would be back next week, meaner than ever, dishing it out, but good, to the yodeling jerk who refused a drink of redeye. You are gone, Charley King, you left us when Richard Widmark pushed the old lady in the wheelchair down the stairs; you are gone and there is no one to replace you.

The films must have been cinematic in the purest sense of the word, since no one ever heard any of the dialogue in the first film on Friday night. There was a solid wall of noise, noise so incredibly loud and enduring, so deafening in its babble of shouts, shrieks and cat-calls from the audience, that it is beyond my power to describe in print. At times the ushers, brave but foolish men, would patrol the aisles, threatening instant exile to any wretch caught causing a disturbance. But it was no use; we were in the Tivoli, we were out of school for the weekend and we were kids. We knew from experience that things would settle down in time for the main feature.

One of the staples, and quite often one of the main features, was a horror movie. How many hours I spent watching the spooky and wonderfully insane antics of George Zucco, Dwight Frye, Lon Chaney, Jr., Ralph Morgan, the immortal Bela Lugosi and the suave, cunning Lionel Atwell, I shall never know. Whatever the figure, they were hours well spent, for within that universe of ghouls and vampires and mad scientists, I found the first signs of order and unity in an art form. The art was a popular art; the order was imposed by second rate artists upon immature minds, and yet . . .

And yet these silly movies contained the outlines of any true work of art. There was a sense of inevitability, an ability to arouse in the spectator primitive emotional responses. The Greeks who watched *Oedipus the King* had at least two things in common with the Tivoli audience watching *Frankenstein;* we both knew the story by heart and we both watched it as if we were seeing it for the first time. Genius and a sense of the eternal forced the Greeks to follow the old, familiar, horrifying story to its bloody end; we, in the Tiv, although we didn't know it at the time, were also in the grip of a great force—the power to obliterate time and space, the power which is so much a part of our century.

Now the important thing about all of this was the effect that these films had on the audience. We had little or no access to other art forms. Like most American children, we had been taught, somewhere, to hate poetry and even anything "poetic." We never knew that the mysterious blend of recorded reality and imagination that was the movies had elements of pure poetry. Reading had too much flavor of school to become a leisure time activity in our crowd. The radio, while a decent enough time-killer, couldn't offer the chance for social intercourse which could be bought for 35 cents at the Tiv.

It was the art of film (though we did not know it then) which made a beach-head—seemingly tenuous, yet there to stay—for the later acceptance of art into our lives. Although I realize that this beach-head did not drive inland into the deeper regions of some of our minds and hearts, it is no exaggeration for me to state that Shakespeare might have died on some heavily guarded parapet of my spirit if Bela Lugosi had not softened up the defenses of ignorance, social conformity, and pure dullness which make up so much of the provincial attitude of the city boy. The movies, even the horror ones, were full of fantasy and incredible happenings and implausible plots and characters.

For this, thank Heavens!

It may seem that the Tiv offered us nothing more than horror and cowboy films. On the contrary, I once saw a Rudolph

Valentino film there, numerous great and near-great films and even "race" films, as I believe they were called. These starred Joe Louis, Ruby Dee, Mantan Moreland and other famous Negro stars and personalities. I also remember seeing what must have been a unique part of cinema history; an all-Negro newsreel. I believe it was called the All-American Newsreel, but since I have never met another person of any color who recalls such films, I hesitate to state that these newsreels really ever did exist or whether I dreamed I saw them.

But all of this is gone now, and if it isn't as romantic as the snows of yesteryear, it is just as important to me. It is all blurring now into some great dream containing other dreams of that time: *Captain Midnight* and *Jack Armstrong* and *I Love a Mystery* and *Allen's Alley* and *Hop Harrigan* on the radio . . . and the *Boy Commandoes* and *The Human Torch* and his sidekick Toro and *Wonder Woman* and the *Green Lantern* and *Doiby Dickles* in the comic books and all the brave young monsters at the Tivoli. I realize now what I should have been doing—according to those who know about what kids should have been doing—I should have been reading Dickens or something of the sort.

But I didn't, and I am glad I didn't because whatever it was I learned from popular culture, whatever it was I learned in that drafty, old building, was important and, in a sense, American. I know now that these things are a part of our heritage, as much as a wastrel nephew may be part of a great family. When I look at popular culture, I look at it not as a critic, but as a friend.

Books

One evening I was standing on the corner when Joe Whritenour gave me a paperback book. What should be remembered here is that this was a time (c. 1950) when "Pocket books," as they were then still called, were considered to be worth discussing only when their covers were lurid. A paperback showing a voluptuous girl with a plunging neckline was reason for a thousand boycotts of a thousand candy stores. When Joe gave me the book I looked at the cover. There was an illustration of a young man standing under a street light. I believe there was a girl standing next to him. He was smoking a cigarette and looking off into the distance. Nothing sexy. The title was *The Young Manhood of Studs Lonigan.* I had never heard of it.

"What's it about?" I asked.

"I don't know, I didn't get into it. It's about New York and the guy hangs out, just like us. You can have it."

I put the book in my jacket pocket and forgot about it. The next day, after school, I began to read it. Joe had, in one way, been wrong. It was about Chicago, not New York. But he had also been right. The guy was like us.

Now, re-reading the Studs Lonigan trilogy with the benefit of hindsight and the scars left from a formal education in English literature, I can see James T. Farrell's great artistic failings. The dialogue is wooden. The characters are one-dimensional. There is no sense of depth. In the words of one of my teachers, reading Farrell is like listening to the creaky, screeching movement of heavy, rusty machinery. Yet, it can be said of *Studs* what Edmund Wilson said of one of the novels of Scott Fitzgerald: It makes every error but one—it doesn't fail to live.

Even now, years after I first sat shattered by my own experience of the shock of recognition, devastated by the truth, the blunt, simple, terrible truth of what Farrell had written—even now, covered with the sludge of the sophistication of taste that comes with formal education and the years, even now Studs Lonigan is alive. He has become, of course, the cliché of Irish-Catholic Americans of my generation. Every boy who has read the book has seen himself as Studs. But Farrell's genius, his ability to transcend his own crippling limitations by writing with a passion and conviction few, if any, contemporary novelists have—this genius has made his novel live.

Anyone who has not read *Studs Lonigan* cannot hope to understand the background from which street corner conservatism originated. Not that Studs' economic and social background was exactly the same as mine, but his psychological and spiritual view of the world was a close reflection of my own and, I suspect, of many in Lafayette who would fall asleep reading *Ivanhoe* but who recognized some dim reflection of their lives in *The Amboy Dukes,* passed around with appropriate "good"—meaning dirty—passages properly earmarked, and who, if they could have gotten through the *Lonigan* trilogy, would have seen that someone, somewhere, knew what it was like to be unsure and to hide behind the Jimmy Cagney tough-guy poses.

It is odd: you can rarely choose the things or the person that make the most dramatic impression on the course of your life. You read a book—and the universe changes. You date a girl and nothing happens. You date her again—and the universe explodes. In my own case how much easier it would be to understand my conservatism if the works of Walter Scott or Coleridge or even Dos Passos had so stunningly changed my life. But they didn't. A tough book written by a tough, Irish-American city-lover did the job. If Farrell has ever come within three light-years of any conservative position, I have never read of it. Yet he knew so very much about us. He knew about the mystery and the wonder of growing up in a city. He knew—and rejected, as did his other great character Danny O'Neill—the kind of absurdity Studs took for granted as a desirable part of life.

Yet Farrell accomplished for me an unintended feat: he managed to make me believe for the first time in my life that a book could be a personal, unique experience. As I have grown older and read more, I have hoped to recapture that sense of discovery, that sense of unexpected, unasked-for joy that I found in reading *Studs*. Alas, the feeling comes only once. But it was enough. Pre-*Studs* I had liked to read (a bit odd in a Lafayette boy as a rule, but forgivable). After *Studs* I became one of the addicted. I went to the library on Pacific Avenue and looked for Farrell's works. None to be found. I stopped off on my way home from school at the main public library downtown where I found a collection of short stories by Farrell. I whisked the book from the shelf as if I had found a first edition.

Even as I read it I knew it wasn't as good as *Studs*—Farrell's limitations as an artist often overcome his enormous, powerful ability to speak from his own heart to that of the reader—but I read it all the way through. I eventually read four or five Farrell books and then tapered off and I have never read one since.

When I had read the last lines of *The Young Manhood of Studs Lonigan* I wanted to cry, so overcome was I by the irony and the realism. But I didn't cry. I just sat there reading over and over the passage about Studs lying in the gutter, Studs who had wanted to be (oh, most dated, and most memorable of phrases) "the real stuff."

So history has its irony: the young, innocent Irish-Catholic boy in Jersey City learns—the way you learn real things, in your heart and in your bones—that books can turn you inside out and upside down, even a book written by an agnostic, former-Catholic, not-quite Marxist, but wholly-socialist, fellow Irish-American. And that knowledge leads the boy to other books in other years, books which, had not the *Lonigan* trilogy made its irrevocable impact, might have slid out of the boy's and, later, the man's consciousness. Because of what Farrell did for me, in later years I was able to learn different, more complex, less immediately enjoyable and understandable, but ultimately more intellectually and spiritually rewarding, lessons from other men and other books.[6]

Jersey City

Jersey City is (a) funny (b) politics (c) dirty.

I learned this growing up there. Mention Jersey City to anyone, anywhere in the United States, and his reaction will be to laugh and say, "Joisey City." The fact of the matter is that no one in Jersey City pronounces it "Joisey." We pronounce it "Jerz."

Jersey City *is* funny, for reasons I have never been able to understand, to most Americans who have heard of it. This may account for the total lack of pride people took in Jersey City when I was a boy. This reluctance to praise Jersey City was, of course, part of the "never-admit-you're-serious" pose so necessary for street corner status. Yet there was something about Jersey City itself which demanded that it not be taken seriously. It was, for one thing, not only notoriously politi-

6. It would seem there is an ethnic barrier when it comes to understanding *Studs Lonigan*. Such thoughtful Jewish intellectuals as Irving Kristol and Nathan Glick have written that the book is (Kristol in *Fortune* magazine): "the description of a Chicago Irish slum" and (Glick in *Dialogue* magazine) that Studs lived in a "Chicago slum." The point to the book—as Farrell made clear in his introduction to the Modern Library Edition (p xii)—is that Studs was not the victim of a slum environment. Studs' Chicago is lace-curtain Irish, respectable, working-class.

cally corrupt but openly and proudly so, and I grew up knowing that so-an-so had a "no-show" job or that my relatives kicked back three percent of their salaries to City Hall and thought nothing of it. Years later, when I visited Saigon, I was briefed by an American Embassy officer on corruption in Vietnam. When he had finished telling me about it I asked if that was all. He seemed shocked. He probably never had come across such governmental corruption before. To someone born and raised in Jersey City, Vietnamese corruption was shocking only in its lack of organization. Give Frank Hague a little room and he would have had Saigon under his thumb and the Viet Cong paid off in five weeks.

In 1949, John V. Kenny, a lieutenant to Boss Frank Hague, rebelled against him. My Uncle John Cummings, who worked in City Hall, was one of the first, if not the first, to wear a Kenny button in City Hall itself. It is difficult to explain just what courage this took. Hague, after all, counted the votes and he had an odd way of counting, always to his own political advantage. The fact that his nephew, Frank Eggers, was Mayor (by decree of Hague) did not matter—everyone knew who was running the city and everyone knew what it meant to cross him.

What my Uncle John did has always remained with me as a symbol of courage. They give no medal for such courage and they don't write profiles in courage about it, but the image of the jaunty little fellow with a Kenny button in his lapel walking up the granite steps of the marvelously grotesque, green-domed City Hall remains for me a supreme act of gallantry. The thin, red line of Englishmen (they were probably Irish, but no matter) who stood their ground at Balaclava showed no greater bravery and fortitude. John V. Kenny won the election, rewarded my uncle with a good job and ward leader's position. In a short while they had, as they say, failed to see eye-to-eye. Uncle Johnnie retired. Kenny remained the boss until the feds caught him years later.

Work

When you got out of high school—one way or the other—you went to work. If you were a male, you worked for Western

Electric in Kearny or Colgates, or you worked downtown, or for the railroad or some insurance company in New York City. If you were female, you worked in New York City as a file clerk or, if you were well-off, attended Katherine Gibbs Secretarial School. Nobody went to college. Nobody even thought of going to college except a few people who didn't know that Real Life meant getting a job, buying new clothes to wear while hanging around, buying a car and going to the drive-in. That was Real Life.

Real Life to me was getting a job in February of 1953 in the Westinghouse Electric Corporation, Elevator and Moving Stairway ("Never say 'escalator'—it's the brand name of the Other Company") Division on Pacific Avenue in Jersey City.

It was all anyone could ask for. Forty-eight fifty a week *to start*, mind you, just like that. They must have been throwing their money away. And, if I woke up early enough—which I rarely did—I could walk the ten or twelve blocks to work and save on carfare. But if I had to get to work in a hurry, I was fortunate enough to be able to catch the Marion-Mallory Avenue bus that passed along Claremont Avenue. It was paradise.

Please don't misunderstand me. I was not the sensitive, young, would-be poet or novelist who took the job for "experience." I took it because I thought that it was all there was. And, in a sense, that *was* all there was. None of my friends attended college. A few, myself included, took a brief pass at Jersey City Junior College, located in Lincoln High School, at nights. But that had a kind of artificial air about it. Real Life was walking through the main entrance of Westinghouse, past the uniformed guard at the desk who took your name if you were even a few seconds late. Real Life meant riding the elevator up the test tower shaft to the blueprint room.

In the blueprint room we made blueprints. We didn't *draw* blueprints—engineers, revered and envied men who worked in another part of the plant, did that, and they were worshipped by young men with ambition—we *made* them, in an ancient machine that caught fire every now and then and had to be drenched with a fire extinguisher. I was a file clerk. I filed the hundreds of blue, glossy originals in our filing cabinets all day while the other young men stood behind the machines feeding the glossies into the machines together with roll upon roll of reproduction paper. Inside the machine some mysterious event took place and out the other side came blueprints. A good machine operator could run the machine and cut the blueprints into appropriate sizes from the long roll.

That was Real Life. In 1955 I entered the Army. In 1957 I had a choice of going back to Westinghouse or going to college. Half-heartedly, and partly because I would get out of the Army almost ninety days early, I chose Jersey City State College.

What would have happened had I returned to Westinghouse? I don't know. For the first semester in Jersey City State College I was miserable. It wasn't Real Life. Real Life was the blueprint room. But it turned out that I didn't go back. It turned out there was another Real Life I never had heard about.

But, for most of my old neighborhood friends and relatives, Real Life *is* the blueprint room or walking a beat or being a fireman or any one of a hundred jobs. I know that life because I lived it—not as some visitor from the intellectual uplands, but as a member of the working force who wanted nothing more—and I know it can be boring and seem to offer nothing but a dead end.

What would I have done had I remained in Westinghouse? I knew and cared nothing about engineering but engineering was the most prestigious field a young man of my age could enter at Westinghouse. Many of my friends went on to become draftsmen and engineers of one sort or another. When would it have occurred to me that my job in Westinghouse was a dead end, that tomorrow was going to be like yesterday which was like each day of all the years before?

I don't know. All I know is that I would have eventually come to the conclusion that I wasn't happy doing what I was doing—or, to be precise, that I would be much happier doing something else. My friends who had different skills and different ideas about happiness went on to different things. Sociologists and liberal intellectuals, bent on belated compassion for urban conservatives, write about the deadly dull routine experience of the blue-collar worker.[7] But what they don't understand is that the deadliness and the dullness, while all too real, are recognized as only a part of life by most workers. It doesn't, contrary to Marxist orthodoxy, distort their entire creative lives—it helps to feed those lives. Whether a man has a workshop at home or goes bowling or goes crabbing with a drop-net at the Jersey shore, he makes his life when he can. If it is off the job, so be it. He knows enough about reality to know that most jobs are dull, dead-end things in themselves. But he doesn't let that fact distort the reality of his own sense of self-worth. When I worked for the Public Service Utilities Company, there was a saying among the meter-readers: "The work is dirty but the money is clean." I think most workers have this attitude. This doesn't mean they are always happy. But it does mean that they are not depressed over their worth to themselves and their families just because they do not fit into some category of Man as Working Creator which is the only kind of life worth living according to many intellectuals.

The dignity of labor is not a myth. But the dignity does not always lie in the labor itself. It lies in the man or woman who is laboring. It lies partially in the fact that he or she has made a compromise, as we all do, between the dream and the reality

7. The Department of Health, Education and Welfare decided to "study the problem" of "alienation." The report, "Work in America," which resulted from that study, was best described by Irving Kristol:

"The document, entitled 'Work in America,' was prepared for HEW by the Upjohn Institute for Employment Research, under the direction of one of its staff, Dr. Harold L. Sheppard. Now, Dr. Sheppard is a most intelligent and thoughtful man, whose competence as a scholar is beyond challenge. But, as it happens, he is also an admirer of Erich Fromm's 'socialist humanism,' and he is sincerely persuaded that the capitalist system 'dehumanizes' its workers because it forces them to sell their labor as a commodity . . .

". . . our upper-middle classes—whose offspring populate the mass media and staff the offices of politicians—have little first-hand knowledge of that world of work which is inhabited by ordinary people. Their heads are full of old and irrelevant stereotypes. Most of them are sincerely convinced, for instance, that Charlie Chaplin's 'Modern Times' gives a true picture of factory work, with the worker forced to become a robot-like slave to the assembly line. Tell them that *fewer than* 2% of American workers are on the assembly line—a fact duly (if fleetingly) recorded in 'Work in America'—and they are incredulous."

—*Wall Street Journal*, January 18, 1973

and, having made that compromise, is willing to do a good job—not for some vague "work ethic"—but for the wife and kids and the new car. These may not be noble ends to some intellectuals, but they are what most urban conservatives think of as the reason for working. The Protestant ethic as such does not flourish in the neighborhoods, but dignity flourishes there with each generation. Some stay with Westinghouse and bring hope and comfort to their families. Some do not stay. But always there is a sense that when you work, whether you are writing a speech or walking a beat, there is a meaning to what you do, maybe not in the job itself but in the good you can get out of the money that comes from the job. The sense of vocation is not limited to the priesthood. To many working men "vocation" means their fatherhood, their duty to family.

In his *The Passing of the Modern Age*,[8] John Lukacs wrote:

> . . . About sixty years ago Charles Peguy wrote that the true revolutionaries of the twentieth century will be the fathers of Christian families. There have been, alas, only too few of them in sight. It is not impossible that the true revolutionaries of the twenty-first century will be the fathers of decent and civilized children . . .

True revolutionaries . . . how seemingly inappropriate a title for the Cummings and the Gavins and the Mikolajczyks and the Gulardis of America. True revolutionaries don't spend their lives hanging around or going to novenas, or taking care of their families and trying their best to get by, taking it day-by-day, trying to get a little more of whatever it is that is out there for their kids.

Yet urban conservatives are, in a way, revolutionaries. They are in undeclared revolt against the dominant philosophy of liberalism that has shaped the cultural and intellectual directions of life in this country for a generation. Their revolution is peaceful because the one thing they are certain of in an increasingly unsure world—where dotty nuns and deranged priests marry, denounce their country and mirthfully flaunt the law—the one thing they are certain of is that this country is too damned good to be burned down or subverted or destroyed. It

8. *The Passing of the Modern Age*, John Lukacs (Harper & Row), p. 82.

is a good country for them and for their kids. And it is precisely because this is a good country that they are revolting against the dominance of liberalism.

Liberalism is, God knows, a complex and difficult concept to pinpoint and almost impossible to define. But the urban conservatives are content to let others do the defining. As for themselves, they have seen the future as liberalism would have it —and they know it doesn't work. All the references in the world to John Stuart Mill aren't going to convince an urban conservative that liberal toleration of the wave of anarchy and violence and campus terror in the late sixties was good for the working man or his family. All the arguments about women's rights, straight from the left-liberal canon, aren't going to convince the guy standing on the corner of Woodward Street and Communipaw Avenue that killing a baby in the womb is a blow for freedom or is justified by some kind of inherent right women have because of the way they are built.

How many such revolutionaries are there? I don't know. How many divisions does the Pope have? It is the same kind of question and arises from the same kind of mentality; pragmatic, political, attuned to only one kind of reality, that of quantitative power. What matters is that a new kind of political reality—a kind of conservatism—is challenging the dominance of liberalism in the cities and in the nation-at-large.

What, then, is this kind of conservatism? It is not Middle-American, a term I always associate with Mom and Pop sitting on the shady porch somewhere in Kansas; it is not ethnic, a term that accentuates origins rather than the principles guiding daily life; it is not hard-hat, although it certainly includes many of those who call themselves that.

It isn't dependent on arguments from free enterprise, although most street corner conservatives embrace free enterprise as being both eminently sensible and demonstrably effective. Neither is it dependent on aristocratic tradition (most street cleaners' sons and grandsons I know don't honor aristocratic traditions to any great extent) nor a particular intellectual viewpoint. If a street corner conservative makes an appeal to philosophic conservative authority for support, it isn't because the authority has convinced him of something but because the authority may provide intellectual proof for something the conservative has known since childhood.

This conservatism is not based on nostalgia for some long-gone golden age nor on some reactionary aesthetic idea which hates the twentieth century of rock music and amplified guitars and X-rated films because it is not the time of the troubadour and the lute.

Perhaps it can best be understood when seen in light of a passage written by John Courtney Murray.[9] Writing in the late nineteen-fifties, he discussed what he saw as a new barbarism. He may well have been writing of the reasons for the growth of a conscious, articulate urban conservatism:

> The barbarian need not appear in bearskins with a club in hand. He may wear a Brooks Brothers suit and carry a ball-point pen with which to write his advertising copy. In fact, even beneath the academic gown there may lurk a child of the wilderness, untutored in the high tradition of civility, who goes busily and happily about his work, a domesticated and law-abiding man, engaged in the construction of a philosophy to put an end to all philosophy, and thus put an end to the possibility of a vital consensus and to civility itself. This is perennially the work of the barbarian, to undermine rational standards of judgment, to corrupt the inherited intuitive wisdom by which the people have always lived, and to do this not by spreading new beliefs but by creating a climate of doubt and bewilderment in which clarity about the larger aims of life is dimmed and the self-confidence of the people is destroyed . . .

The undermining of rational standards of judgment has been, and is now, an important part of intellectual life in the United States. The street corner conservative who goes to college comes face-to-face with this new kind of barbarism which seeks to "corrupt the inherited intuitive wisdom." One goal of the street corner conservative is to uphold rational standards of judgment against debasement by current non-rational and even anti-rational philosophies. He finds he cannot do this by relying on the liberalism which so comforted his Catholic in-

9. *We Hold These Truths*, John Courtney Murray, S.J., p. 12, Sheed and Ward, Inc., 1960.

tellectual cousin in the fifties. Liberalism has failed to combat the debasement of reason and it has done so precisely because, in and of itself, it offers no defense against this debasement and, indeed, has contributed to it. As John Courtney Murray wrote:

> The barbarian may be the eighteenth-century philosopher, who neither anticipated nor desired the brutalities of the Revolution with its Committee on the Public Safety, but who prepared the ways for the Revolution by creating a vacuum which he was not able to fill. Today the barbarian is the man who makes open and explicit rejection of the traditional role of reason and logic in human affairs. He is the man who reduces all spiritual and moral questions to the test of practical results or to an analysis of language or to decision in terms of individual subjective feeling . . .

I am certain that liberal professors in the fifties and early sixties neither anticipated nor desired the brutalities of the late sixties, but they prepared the way by creating a vacuum they were not able to fill.

The liberals' love affair with "the test of practical results" led us into urban chaos and, I believe, into the incredible series of maneuvers and strategies that made the Vietnam War one of the most agonizing experiences in American history. The guy on the street corner knows that spiritual and moral questions are not answered by analyzing language or in terms of subjective feeling. That is why he, for the most part, has been in the forefront of the drives against what is called "permissiveness" and against drug abuse. Street corner conservatives want to bring to the center of public decision-making the spiritual and moral values of Western civilization, values that have been either ignored or misinterpreted by liberal politicians and academics.

> . . . Barbarism threatens when men cease to live together according to reason, embodied in law and custom, and incorporated in a web of institutions that sufficiently reveal rational influences, even though they are not, and cannot be, wholly rational. Society becomes barbarian when men are huddled together under the rule of force and fear; when economic interests assume the primacy over higher values; when material

> standards of mass and quantity crush out the values of quality and excellence; when technology assumes an autonomous existence and embarks on a course of unlimited self-exploitation without purposeful guidance from the higher disciplines of politics and morals (one thinks of Cape Canaveral); when the state reaches the paradoxical point of being everywhere intrusive and also impotent, possessed of immense power and powerless to achieve rational ends; when the ways of men come under the sway of the instinctual, the impulsive, the compulsive. When things like this happen, barbarism is abroad, whatever the surface impressions of urbanity. Men have ceased to live together according to reasonable laws . . .

Street corner conservatism is in rebellion against the state being everywhere, at once intrusive and impotent—a precise definition of the New Frontier and the Great Society. "Programmatic" liberalism, whether it is of the Ripon Society or the Brookings Institution-type, has been at the center of most political decision-making in the United States for the past twenty years. The street corner conservative wants to take a long, hard look at "programs" of any type, especially those which promise him and his family instant utopia. He has been burned, quite literally in the case of urban and campus riots, once too often and from now on he wants a say in determining what direction the nation is going to take. For too long he has been told to depend on Harvard-types, either Republican or Democrat, to do his thinking for him. He has seen the results of their thinking and he has decided to do some thinking of his own.

> . . . Barbarism likewise threatens when men cease to talk together according to reasonable laws. There are laws of argument, the observance of which is imperative if discourse is to be civilized. Argument ceases to be civil when it is dominated by passion and prejudice; when its vocabulary becomes solipsist, premised on the theory that my insight is mine alone and cannot be shared; when dialogue gives way to a series of monologues; when the parties to the conversation cease to listen to one another, or hear only what they want to hear, or see the other's argument only through the screen of their own categories; when defiance is flung to the basic ontological principle of all

> ordered discourse, which asserts that Reality is an analogical structure, within which there are variant modes of reality, to each of which there corresponds a distinctive method of thought that imposes on argument its own special rules. When things like this happen, men cannot be locked together in argument. Conversation becomes merely quarrelsome or querulous. Civility dies with the death of the dialogue . . .

The principles that informed John Courtney Murray's description of the new barbarism are at the very center of street corner conservatism. "The death of civility" is not just a high-sounding phrase to the urban conservatives. Urban violence has always been with us. But for the first time in history we have a kind of urban violence that not only harms the victim but claims that he is guilty of the crime at the same time. Elizabethan London had its muggers, I am sure. But if someone had said to a bleeding and dazed Elizabethan mugging victim that it was his fault that the knave walloped him, I'm certain there would have been swordplay in the streets as soon as the victim recovered.

Yet, during the nineteen-sixties not a day passed when some liberal politician did not decry violence out of one side of his mouth and, out of the other, blame the working-class victims for bringing about the conditions that led the mugger to mug. Behind the politician's rhetoric was the philosophical barbarism of the intellectual élite in the United States.

It is easy to dismiss urban conservatism as simply a reactionary movement which will fade as soon as the crime index goes down a few points. I think, however, that although the genesis of urban conservatism may be found in a reaction against physical and moral violence, its continuing strength lies in other areas. The Archie Bunker kind of bitterness, fear and bigotry which is often seen as a precise description of the values of urban conservatives is only a part—and I think a small part—of what is happening to urban conservatism. Reaction to violence and neglect made many urban conservatives conscious of their conservatism. Now that they are conscious of it, the abundance of moral strength, patriotism and love of family that typifies the street corner conservative will be directed into new, constructive channels.

Out of the lives of the people I have described—my family, my friends, the people of Lafayette and downtown and, now, of the suburbs in New Jersey and elsewhere—out of their lives and the lives of others like them across the nation has come a great power that is never seen on the television screens, never discussed in the colleges, never really understood by most political figures. This is a power that is part serenity, part courage, part, yes, patience and long-suffering, unfashionable as these virtues may seem in an age of instant envy and well-rewarded public rages. Such power is made of long summer evenings spent hanging around on corners or in bars, talking quietly, having a few beers, playing darts; it is a power gained by working day after day and going to church on Sunday and making sure the kids do what's right; it is the kind of power that comes from bed-rock belief in traditional virtues and in the concept of God that has been either openly mocked or subtly ridiculed by many major institutions—including, alas, even the churches in some cases—during the past dozen or so years. Some say that this power doesn't exist. But I know better. I have been fortunate enough to have my life touched by it and I know that the street corner conservatism it flows from is going to transform this country.

Chapter 2
The Fantasy Continues

At this point in my fantasy I pause. Around the long conference table, the media moguls and newspaper nabobs who have been patiently listening, now want to ask questions.

Q. Let me get this straight. Is this a pitch for another quota system? Do you want a certain number or percentage of your kind of people hired by the government or accepted into Ivy League universities? Is this what all this yelling and screaming is about? The alleged unfairness of what you call "liberal dominance"?

A. I can understand that after fifteen years of having people scream at you, demanding this and that, you probably have difficulty in believing that there are people who can be mad at you, but not want something from you. No, we don't want quotas of any kind.

Q. You seem to imply that your kind of conservatism has some real intellectual base to it. I hate to say this, but it sounds to me like the same old Holy-Mother-Church-Knows-Best argument, the kind we used to hear from Catholics who wanted to show that they had all the answers. All of that stuff has been discredited. Can you name one non-Catholic thinker who takes all of this seriously?

A. You're asking a question that is in itself part of the problem. You're absolutely correct. It would be difficult to find many of any intellectual standing in the United States who would accept my premise which is, in part at least, that those ways of looking at the world we call liberalism are inferior to those ways of looking at the world I call conservatism. I hold that liberalism is an intellectual system that has demonstrably failed—on its own terms. I further hold that conservatism has not so much been discredited as ignored or made to seem part of an esoteric creed understood only by certain readers of *National Review*. No, my kind of conservatism—while it exists and lives day by day in the viscera of most of our people—does have an intellectual base with legitimate claim to a true intellectual heritage. It can be applied today to help this country.

Q. That's all a bit vague. Give me an example.

A. All right. Look, on the most basic level you can't make major political decisions without making a moral decision of some kind. If you make moral decisions, you have to base them on something, some standard. Will someone please tell me what moral standard liberalism provides? Moral relativism used to be a catch phrase used by conservative intellectuals to scare liberals. But now we see that moral relativism can have concrete results. Look at the nineteen-sixties and Watergate for details.

Q. Oh, come off it! Are you saying that everything that went wrong in the late sixties—and, by the way, a hell of a lot went right that you just conveniently happened to forget—are you saying all that went wrong is the fault of liberalism?

A. Just about. Think for a minute. When the sixties began, liberalism was triumphantly in the lead. In the ten years that have since passed this country almost fell apart and we still haven't recovered. Now, when a philosophy has all the political power, complete control of the mass media and unchallenged dominance in intellectual life, isn't it reasonable to blame that philosophy when things go wrong? You can't have it both ways. If liberalism means anything at all, it means a commitment to finding solutions to the problems of this world. By any standard, American liberalism failed in the sixties; its failure was basic and irrevocable because it failed when it was in possession of almost total power.

Q. I hope I'm wrong . . . but could you possibly be referring obliquely to that old spook "natural law"? Not *that* one again!

A. It's a fault I share with, among others, Walter Lippmann (see his *The Public Philosophy*). Now look, I'm not saying I can, here and now, begin to give an explanation of how adherence to the concept of natural law would improve, say, the crime problem in Washington, D.C. But I *am* saying that intelligent men who have long neglected that concept, or laughed at it out of court, should re-examine it. I'm sure they will find that men and women all over this nation try to live by its precepts, even if they can't fully explain it.

Q. Let me get back to what you're trying to do here. Is this another one of those "we-can-save-America" acts? James Baldwin pulled it off rather well in *The Fire Next Time*. You know, we are a despised group but it is only through us that the rest of you can achieve salvation. It's a spin-off of the old Marxist belief in the ability of the despised proletariat to "save" the capitalist even if it destroys the capitalist culture.

Are you trying to tell us that these street corner conservatives are going to save America from liberalism through great applications of scholastic philosophy?

A. No. Most of those I'm talking about never heard of scholastic philosophy. And few of them are concerned with saving anything except, perhaps, souls (theirs, not yours) and some money. No, we don't expect to save society. All we ask is that those who dominate the intellectual, cultural and social life of this nation stop destroying what we have here. And don't kid yourself: liberalism has been destroying our little piece of this nation. Not through malice but through sheer liberal good will. We can't afford any more liberal good will. It comes at a very high cost to us. No, we don't give a damn if you are saved or not. We just want you to stop doing to us what you have been doing to us for a generation. We're sick of it all.

Q. Is this a call for a new political party?

A. No. The last thing we want is a third or fourth or fifth party along rigid, doctrinaire, ideological lines. We want to continue to work through the two-party system. Unfortunately, the Democratic party has for the past ten years forgotten us and the move to the Republican party has been complicated for many of us by traditional distrust of the GOP as the party of business, not to mention Watergate. Thus, a guy like George Wallace could gain a great part of our support while the rest might either stay in the Democratic party through inertia or else move to vote for one-shot Republican candidates, e.g., Nixon in 1972. The big job during the next few years will be for the Republican party to show us that it is prepared to accept us on our terms (which would mean, at the very least, some power for us in party decisions) or for the Democratic party to change its ways. One alternative seems as unlikely as the other at this point.

Q. Isn't this merely another version of the "deprived minority" routine we've heard so often in recent years? Every month or so someone announces that his particular group has been a victim of society or Amerika or the liberals or the establishment or the white man or big business or something. By talking about street corner conservatives, aren't you simply trying to get into the act?

A. I agree with you that we tend to have a Gripe-of-the-Month Club in this country. But I can't help that. Some gripes happen to be real. I think that the basic difference between the people I'm talking about and the people you're talking about is that my people are not asking for or demanding anything or claiming that they've been given a raw deal from the beginning. Hell, we always loved this country and all we ask is that we get the chance to live our lives the way we want to.

Nobody is talking about "fire next time" or "revolution in the streets." We don't want anything; we just want to get by. But everywhere we look, the most powerful elements in society are not only neglecting our values but actively working against them. The street corner conservatives don't want more federal money or more federal jobs or dinner invitations to the White House. We want the current onslaught against our values to stop. We want the old radical-chic crowd to know that, when it indulges in its social and political fantasies, it usually happens that the workingman and his family get hurt. The children of the middle and upper-middle class made the mess at Woodstock and other festivals; the children of urban conservatives cleaned it up. The kids who rioted in the streets in Chicago were your kids; the cops who stopped them were ours. The kids who began the campus disturbances of the sixties were your kids; the kids who either were fooled into following them or who tried to keep the schools open were ours. You said our country was morally wrong in Vietnam; we knew it wasn't. As you can see, your view, the dominant intellectual view, the mass media view, isn't ours.

Q. If you don't mind my saying so, you seem terribly defensive. All this nasty talk about liberalism and how it has hurt you. Could it be that you're simply jealous of the enormous success and prestige that liberalism has achieved? Could it be that your people—and you—would like very much to adopt a liberal way of life but just can't manage it? Could it be that you have what used to be called an inferiority complex and are trying to destroy liberalism, not because it is bad, but because it is obviously superior to anything your street corner conservatism has ever produced?

A. Being jealous of the success of contemporary liberalism would be something like being jealous of the success of Typhoid Mary. No, we don't envy Punch Sulzberger, we pity him. Your last point is, however, well taken. We do at times feel inferior. And why shouldn't we? You control every major intellectual and cultural institution of this nation. You control the universities, the networks, the big publishing houses, the news magazines. You hire people who, for various reasons, choose to see things through your eyes. We are inundated every day with your view of the world. Little wonder we have come to feel that our view is not only unreported but somehow wrong. Hell, even when you *do* hire some of our people—Jimmy Breslin comes to mind, and Pete Hamill—it's only because they resemble your vision of us in the same way that Stepin Fetchit resembled your vision of the black man only a few decades ago. It is easy and comfortable for you to think of us as wild, blowzy, booze-swilling, vulgar, sloppy buffoons or as hot-tempered, wild-eyed zealots whose ideas are all in their guts. But, the Breslins and Hamills not only play the role you want them to play to your vast amusement, but never dare to go beyond the ideological limits your dominance assigns to them. They never really question any of *your* broad assumptions. In fact, they embrace them. Their view of the Vietnam War was not, repeat not, the view of the average guy in Queens, Breslin to the contrary notwithstanding. The guy in Queens didn't like the war, but only because we didn't blast the hell out of our enemies right away. All of that *New York Post-New York Magazine* nonsense that Breslin and Hamill spout is simply another version of your basic line. These guys speak with the true accent of our people but the only reason you tolerate them is that they never have deviated from liberal dogma in all the years they have been published.

Sure, you know some guys from my background but they are not conservatives; you know some conservatives but they're not from my background. Therefore, our point of view never gets on the air or in popular print. And it should. For one thing, it's different from the usual pap you fellows put out. And while it's conservative, it doesn't sound like Bill Buckley who, bless his soul, wouldn't know how to hang around if his life depended on it.

Q. We're getting nowhere. One final question: Why the hell do you invite us to your fantasies, if you think we're all such a bunch of bastards?

A. You've got me there. It's true that while I don't like liberalism, I like many liberals. Look, I was educated, at public expense, in a state teachers college and I'm always yelling about how I received a liberal indoctrination. Well, it's true. But it is also true that the teachers at Jersey City State College were superb in their dedication to teaching and in their patience and in their help. I owe them a debt I can never repay. So don't tell me that I'm contradicting myself by damning you and inviting you to my fantasies. Can I help it if what you taught me helped me to discover that what you believe is wrong?

Chapter 3

A Conservative's Liberal Education

Street corner conservatism is for me based on the discovery, in my college years but not in college classes, that those unarticulated political and social beliefs of my working class, Catholic family were not the foolish superstitions liberal college professors believed them to be. Instead, I discovered them as simple and specific examples of the complex and universal principles which are at the root of order and progress in the Western world. It might best be put this way: Although it is highly unlikely that my parents or grandparents ever heard of, let alone read, C. S. Lewis or Frank Meyer, the general philosophy of my grandparents' lives had its foundation in the basic principles articulated by these great champions of philosophical conservatism.

In discovering I was a conservative, I found I was reaffirming in a different, more complicated way, the barely understood, never discussed, but always present philosophical premises that were held by my family and my friends and my neighborhood in Jersey City.

G. K. Chesterton once wrote that there are two ways of getting home. One is to go all around the world until you come to it. The other is to stay there in the first place. Many street corner conservatives have moved, geographically, to the suburbs. But philosophically and spiritually we have stayed home. It is a good place to be. Yet, because of the peculiar and ubiquitous nature of the dominant liberal philosophical viewpoint in the United States, it is difficult, almost impossible, for the average, young, intelligent, urban conservative to grasp the very fact that he not only *is* conservative, but, by right, ought to be.

The liberals in politics, in the academies, in the best magazines are, I think, mostly decent, fair-minded men and women but because of the dominant and, paradoxically enough, restrictive nature of contemporary liberalism, they have a difficult time realizing that there are other than liberal ways—and those left-of-center ideologies liberalism tolerates and protects and patronizes—of looking at the world. Confronted by a claim that conservatism is the true, indeed the only, logical philosophical posture of millions of urban Americans, some liberals go into culture shock.

I discovered this in 1961, my senior year at Jersey City State College, when I represented my school on a local television program during which students from the New Jersey state colleges were to question then-Governor Robert Meyner in a Meet-the-Press format. Before the program began, we met briefly with Meyner and I happened to mention to him a policy then advocated by Barry Goldwater. Meyner leaned across the table and, with evident concern, said: "But . . . you're not one of his followers, are you?"

I mumbled that, well, gee, you might say that; I do, sort of, like some of the things Barry says. Meyner stared at me for a second or two. He didn't grimace or blink or even shake his head. He just stared. He was probably wondering how a denizen of Jersey City could embrace any of Goldwater's policies.

It was, to him, a sin against nature, Northern New Jersey-style.

Before and since that meeting with Meyner, I have been asked how anyone who comes from my kind of background—who was born and raised in Jersey City, who for eighteen years lived in city neighborhoods integrated to a degree that would have delighted the heart of Eleanor Roosevelt, and one whose life was changed at the age of sixteen upon discovering the works of James T. Farrell—in short, how anyone like me can be a real conservative.

Yet, looked at from another viewpoint, the question itself is puzzling. Many liberals say: What else would you expect a working class Irish-Catholic from Jersey City to be *but* conservative? It is universally agreed that the Irish-Catholic working class is the most notoriously conservative group in the country.

Father Andrew Greeley, the prolific and talented sociologist, is one who disagrees with the Irish-Catholic conservative thesis.[10] He calls it one of the great myths of "pop" social science and produces charts based on data gathered by the National Opinion Research Center to show that the Irish "may be as liberal as, if not more so than, the rest of the American gentile population on questions of race and war." The Irish, he writes, "have voted for liberal Democratic presidential candidates for four decades." Father Greeley's reputation as an outstanding sociologist and my own total ineptitude in the field seem to leave me with little choice but to accept his findings. Yet, there is a sentence in the book which strongly suggests that, to Father Greeley, "liberal" and "conservative" are not only sociological labels but terms of value as well. "To those who accuse the Irish of being conservative," he writes, "one might reply by pointing to the Irish contribution to the development of the labor movement . . ."

Doth he protest too much? Why is the labeling of Irish-Catholics as conservatives seen by Father Greeley as an accusation? My dictionary defines "accusation" as a "charge of wrongdoing; imputation of guilt or blame." What Father Greeley is saying, in effect, is that his liberal colleagues have found the Irish in

10. *That Most Distressful Nation* (Quadrangle, 1972), pp. 216-222.

America guilty of conservatism but he feels all the evidence is not yet in, much of it is circumstantial, and he seems to be saying: "Anyhow, my client was home that evening and we have witnesses to prove it."

My own view is that the Irish in America, at times a cantankerous people, do not fit easily into either the "conservative" or "liberal" category. "Conservatism" does, to most people, have connotations of stuffiness, arrogance, humorlessness and dullness with which, even by the strongest efforts of the imagination, we find it hard to associate the Irish. As for the liberals, especially the intellectuals, Father Greeley neatly delineates the Irish attitude toward them:

> There seems to be a grudging reluctance on the part of American intellectuals to face the horrors of the Famine, the perils of the North Atlantic crossing, and the inhuman experiences of the emigrant Irish. Indeed, one finds precious little compassion for the Irish either in contemporary accounts of the early years of immigration or in present reflections upon those years. I am unaware of a single American intellectual who ever bothered to try to understand the present state of the American Irish in terms of their past experiences. The Irish have never been an approved object of sympathy or understanding in the American Republic. It is perhaps just as well, because at this point in time we are capable of declaring ourselves able to do without the intellectuals' compassion, sympathy, and understanding; we made it in spite of their hatred and oppression. There lurks in the Irish psyche, I am convinced, a profound skepticism about the fashionable compassions of the American liberal do-gooder. We are inclined to think their compassions are just a bit phony, and we wonder where they were when we needed their help. We also find it just a bit ironic when they demand that we feel guilty for what their ancestors did to the blacks and the American Indians. They do not seem to display much guilt for what happened to us at the hands of their ancestors here and in Europe.

All the sociological data in the world are not going to convince people—least of all the Irish—that the Irish are liberals. Yet, I must admit that to call them conservative seems to be either twisting the language or misreading reality as much on one side as the liberal sociologists do on the other. Who can imagine an Irish-Catholic Robert Taft?

Still, it is "urban conservative" and "street corner conservative" which I have chosen as labels for those white, ethnic, blue-collar workers who live in the cities and for their children and grandchildren who, despite the fact that they now have attended college and live in the suburbs, continue to look at the world in much the same way their fathers and grandfathers always have. If "conservative" does not seem to fit these people, the fault is in the way people use the word, not in the behavior and the attitude of the Irish (and, I think, of practically all the other ethnic groups) in America.

If, indeed, conservatism is something one is accused of, like shop-lifting or bad breath, then the Irish, I hope, are not conservative. But if it refers to certain philosophical and social ways of looking at the world, then the Irish may apply for the conservative label and do so with good reason. To dismiss the Irish as not being conservative—because their life-style in America does not resemble that of, say, a laissez-faire economist of the Ayn Rand school or a little old lady in tennis shoes in Orange County, California—is to deprive them of what, I think, is a legitimate and even proud title . . . just because others who have laid claim to that title (or, more often, have had it pinned on them by those in whose political interest it was to make conservatism seem narrow or regional or a bit nutty) often differ from the Irish in basic attitudes and behavior.

Concerning the kind of conservatism typical of the Irish in America, I think the following points can be made:

1. Its basis is neither political nor economic, but philosophical. Generally speaking, the Irish in America look at the world in a way that liberals can neither understand nor, when the crunch comes, tolerate. If liberalism means anything at all, it means, in the United States during the twentieth century, a predilection for big, centralized government in politics, for experimentation and "innovation" in education, for on-going and detailed criticism of organized religion, for relativism in morality, for a view of the world stressing the general, the abstract and the mass as opposed to the specific, the concrete and the individual.

While it is risky, if not downright dangerous, to make generalizations about the attitude of the Irish-Americans toward government, I think it is safe to say that the "profound skepticism" of which Father Greeley writes focuses not only on the liberal intellectuals but on the various political programs and policies that have evolved from liberal intellectual initiatives. This skepticism is not directed toward "liberals" as people, but to the ideas (a) that the world and man's role in it are capable of being understood by reason alone, (b) that the tragedies of mankind can be reduced, through slide-rules, computers and round-table seminars of Ivy League professors to "problems" that can be "solved" and (c) that a man's chief glory is to bring about change, to make things "better" for "society."

The Irish do not really care that much about "society" in the sociological sense of the word, and they never have, being too busy working to help their families survive and, with God's help, prosper. The do-goodism of the liberal is not simply a kind of quirk which can be wished away, leaving liberalism open to the Irish mind and heart. Such obsession with the betterment of others through government *is* liberalism or, at any rate, has been for fifty years or more and the Irish in America, as a group, have not been a part of it.

To state, as Father Greeley does, that the existence of Irishmen in the labor movement is proof of their liberalism is, once more, arbitrarily to assign to "conservatism" an anti-union bias which is simply not there. The uncompelled joining together of workers to help them get from their employers the best possible economic terms is not a "liberal" idea. Certainly, it is not an idea held exclusively by liberals. That many conservatives have shown an anti-union bias is, of course, true, but I hold this to be proof that many conservatives misunderstand conservatism. The Irish who led the union fights were not doing it because of some liberal vision of abstract justice. They were doing it because they felt they were not getting paid what they should for their labor. This is something that no Irishman is going to take sitting down—unless, of course, he is sitting down to strike. The specific and concrete good of his family and their ability to rise in the world was the reason the Irish led the battles for the unions.

There is currently a kind of nostalgic longing among the liberal intellectuals for the good old days when the Irishman knew his place and voted the right way. This nostalgia, like all nostalgia, colors and distorts reality. The Irish in America have never had anything in common with the liberal vision of do-goodism. The only good the average Irish-American has sought to do has been to his own family or his church. If, in the process, he helped liberal causes it was a by-product of his major effort. It is impossible to conceive of a liberal during the past twenty-five years or so who hasn't embraced the doctrine of "do-goodism," which usually means we will do good to you, so shut up. It is equally impossible to think of this kind of do-goodism among the urban Irish-Americans. This lack of do-goodism may, in some eyes, make the Irish seem less than noble. But nobility, after all, has never been much esteemed by the Irish.

2. The Irishman's view of America has been, for the most part, a pleasantly uncomplicated one: he likes it. Once more, he has, in his perversity, gone against the liberal strain. Criticism of the United States has been a trademark of liberalism for many years, most evidently so during the last decade. Genocidal abroad, and at home exploitative of the downtrodden and the oppressed: that has been the image of America the Ugly as seen through left-liberal eyes. This does not discount the Molly McGuires and the draft riots of the Civil War or other manifestations of Irish discontent. I am not saying the Irish were never unhappy in America, only that there has never been an Irish world-view that held America in contempt.

To the Irish-American who was beginning to make it in the coarse, materialistic way so loathed by liberal pundits, this was, and is, a good country. His kids were going to college, he was making a little bit more, his wife had a new coat, they got away to the shore every summer—it wasn't perfect but it was good. But "good" wasn't good enough for the liberals. And so the Irish-American's genuine and outspoken love of this country clashed with his former political master's harangues about what was wrong with this country.

There has been similar, strictly conservative criticism of the United States but, once more, the Irish were not that kind of conservative. That conservative criticism looked upon America and found her gross (no culture worth speaking of except, perhaps, for Ezra Pound), dying (the whole universe has been winding down since the thirteenth, greatest of centuries) and not worth saving (let us go across the river and rest in the shade of our I-told-you-so's). The Irish-American has not seen the nation this way. He knows America has problems but that it is also far superior to any existing nation and to any nation of history, and he knows a good thing when he sees one.

3. There is, of course, that Irish-American prejudice against Communism. It has been severely censured by liberal wisemen who have told us that the road to Hell is paved with anti-Communism. It would appear that the Nixon trips to Peking and Moscow would have brought forth a cry from the Irish-American community. They brought forth, for the most part, the same kind of reaction usually given to professional football games on television; they were fun to watch and read about but nothing to get excited about after they were over. Yet, to state that this response meant approval of the long-time liberal rationale for détente-at-any-cost with the Communist world is silly. The trips themselves, if not their theatrical style, were seen for what they were: shrewd politics, and there is nothing an Irishman admires as much as shrewd politics, the shrewder the better.

The average Irish-American, if asked, would have stated his dislike of American involvement in Vietnam, but mainly because we had not bombed the hell out of the Communists a long time ago. In his view, the immorality of the war, if there was any, was in sending in Americans to try to do piecemeal what should have been done quickly, massively and decisively. If, indeed, this could not be done, why were we there in the first place? Out of the mouths of urban Irishmen oft come gems. If you're going to fight someone, fight him; if you are not, don't. Perhaps the Harvard intellectuals who pushed America into gradualism would have benefitted from a talk with the boys on the street corner.

4. The average Irish-American has a peculiar intellectual disability as far as liberal intellectuals are concerned. He can't seem to get it through his head that rape and murder and mugging are signs of social protest arising from unwarranted social conditions for which the Irish-American is to blame. He still thinks that rape is rape, murder is murder and mugging is

mugging, intellectually disreputable as such simplistic thinking may appear. His view arises not from the aftereffects of a jesuitical, new-Aristotelian education in logical thought, but from deep conviction drilled into him by his parents and by traditional nuns and by experience that these things are bad in and of themselves and that, if he commits one of them, he is (a) guilty in the eyes of man and (b) sinful in the eyes of God. Guilt, to liberals in recent years, means what they determine others are supposed to feel because, three hundred years ago, black men sold other black men to white men who transported them in chains across the ocean. Sin, of course, is a concept not within the range of the liberal mind. So the Irish-American urban conservative's view of what urban violence means does not, and quite naturally cannot, co-exist with the liberal doctrine.

In the good old days of the sixties, when the liberals were equating law and order with racism (who can forget the "code word" ploy?), they were shocked to find that those who had voted for Bobby Kennedy in the 1968 primaries were, in many cases, the same people who supported George Wallace. Trying to explain this seeming anomaly became a small industry among liberals. It was finally decided that the same white urban worker who voted for Bobby, but who also supported George, was showing that, deep down, he was liberal and simply waiting for a good liberal to come along. What the liberal failed to understand was that the man who voted for Bobby, and who also liked George, was not doing anything but voting for the guy he thought could best clean up the urban mess, i.e., get tough with law breakers.

It wasn't the "compassionate" Bobby of the liberal myth for whom the blue-collar workers voted, but the "ruthless" Bobby, the tough-on-crime, bitter, determined little bastard who nailed Jimmy Hoffa. They didn't vote for Bobby because Bobby got a nice press from liberal journalists with stars in their eyes (nowhere in American political literature can one find a more sugar-coated version of reality than in the books that were written about Bobby Kennedy after his death; by comparison even the JFK-as-saint hagiologists were muckrakers). They voted for him because he looked and sounded like the kind of guy who would "put them (the lawbreakers) in their place." The voters were, of course, fooled about Bobby; but so were the liberals who thought they had discovered a new or reborn trend toward liberalism among urban ethnic types, including the Irish. The nomination of Senator George McGovern and his subsequent catastrophe put a damper, for the time being, on the theory that the Irish were lusting for a liberal presidential candidate.

No, I think that the folk-wisdom in this case tells us more about reality than do the sociological data, imposing though they might be. Most of us do tend to think of Irish-Catholics as conservative in political and social outlook. Why, then, is it so surprising to find the son of a quintessential Irish-Catholic, working class family and background who claims to be a conservative?

I think the question must be answered in two ways. First, there should be nothing at all surprising about an Irish-Catholic being conservative. But it is surprising, I believe, to find an Irish-Catholic calling himself "a" conservative. There is all the difference in the world between "conservative" and "*a* conservative." The former describes a set of social and religious and philosophical viewpoints held by certain people; the latter signifies that those viewpoints are held consciously, deliberately, after study and investigation and can, for the most part, be articulated.

My mother and father and grandparents on both sides are conservative; I am "a" conservative. This does not mean "a" conservative is more-right-wing-than-thou. It means that, instead of taking the usual roads open to those who come from conservative backgrounds and who have intellectual aspirations, "a" conservative chooses another road.

The first road open to most young Catholic, intellectually-oriented men and women of my generation was the "Catholic-but-liberal" road. This has been described—and mercilessly, if hilariously, dissected—by Garry Wills in his *Bare Ruined Choirs,*[11] as the world of "Fifties Catholicism: Gregorian Chants and Encyclicals." He writes:

> When liberals of the forties and fifties spoke of a Catholic ghetto, they did not mean the racial or economic kind (though some of

11. *Bare Ruined Choirs* (Doubleday, 1972), pp. 38-60.

their immigrant forefathers had lived in such enclaves, apart from respectable American life). It was the ghetto mentality they referred to, an isolation from the intellectual currents of this country, from the "right" schools and fashionable journals. Breaking out of such a ghetto was the task of intellectuals, and no project had higher priority with liberals of that era than the formation of a body of intellectuals. Would-be sophisticates called out wistfully for one another. Mutual exhortations to "be sophisticated" were urgently, often naively, issued—young collegians encouraging each other (in effect) to read a dirty book for God.

This was the world of *Commonweal* and *The Catholic Worker*, of Gene McCarthy[12] and Thomas Merton, of liturgical reform and the crusade against Joe McCarthy, of the magazine *America* reading William F. Buckley, Jr. out of the church, and as Wills puts it, a "search for steel and glass, fish-shaped churches, and drift-wood swirl Madonnas and wrought-iron abstract tracery for the Stations of the Cross (artily photographed in *Jubilee*)."

There was a second road, however, (and a second way to explain my own conservatism) for young Catholics who didn't want to get bogged down in the aesthetics-and-social-doctrine world of the "Catholic-but-liberals." This was the "liberal-but-Catholic" road and it opened, for the most part, with the nomination and election of John F. Kennedy. Wills writes:

> In all this the Catholic liberal remained on easy shared ground with non-Catholics of the time. Arthur Schlesinger and others singled out Kennedy's secularity as his outstanding virtue. Liberals of the *Encounter* persuasion had proclaimed an "end of ideology," and Kennedy was the kind of "problem solver" required in such a value-free world of non-theoretical concerns. According to his Harvard professor of politics, he treated questions of state, "like a young scientist in the laboratory." He shunned ideological terms just as much as he did the religious label. Asked whether he meant to be a conservative or a liberal as President, he answered, "I hope to be responsible"—a realist, what his wife called, "an idealist without illusions."

12 His wife's entertaining and enlightening *Public Places, Private Faces* gives an inside view of what it was like to be a fifties liberal Catholic.

Perhaps the most prominent and successful example of the "liberal-but-Catholic" road is Daniel Patrick Moynihan. This does not mean that Moynihan's Catholicism is in some way tainted by his amazing success in both the academy and government, but that most observers tend to think of him as a liberal scholar who happens to be Catholic rather than, as was the case in the past with many prominent Catholic intellectuals, as a Catholic who dabbles successfully in liberal politics. Moynihan is Catholic but unobtrusively so, and even though he has had traffic with the devil (former President Nixon) he was once among the saints (the New Frontier) and his recent sins, if not yet forgiven, are capable of absolution by the Higher Liberals because he has loved, at the right time, the right things. Moynihan is witty, intelligent and has progressed along the road of the "liberal-but-Catholic" about as far as anyone can.

Now, in my own case, the first road was never really open because it depended, for the most part, upon a Catholic education. I left the Catholic educational system in 1952, with the completion of four years in Saint Michael's High School, the kind of place against which the "Catholic-but-liberal" intellectual was rebelling. For twelve years I had been taught by the Sisters of Charity, an order then not known for innovation or rebellion of any sort, although I fear that nineteen-sixties type "innovation" has come, alas, even to this teaching order.

After high school graduation I went to work as a clerk in the Westinghouse Elevator Division on Pacific Avenue in Jersey City, hardly a place where Gene McCarthy-type Catholic intellectuals congregate, then or now.

Accordingly, I missed all of the aesthetics and social doctrine ("My encyclical is better than your encyclical") controversies that marked the world of the "Catholic-but-liberal." I was still a parish-oriented, Rosary-saying, confession-going Catholic with the world view of a provincial city boy. As for the second road, I didn't take that because by the time John F. Kennedy was nominated I had already voted for one Republican president and, during the interval between 1956, when I was still in the Army, and 1960, something happened.

What happened was that I became aware of the conservative movement, not through a book or an idea or a philosophical theory—but a person.

> The heart is commonly reached, not through the reason, but through the imagination, by means of direct impressions, by the testimony of facts and events, by history, by description. Persons influence us, voices melt us, looks subdue us, deeds inflame us. Many a man will live and die upon a dogma; no man will be a martyr for a conclusion . . .
>
> No great work was ever done by a system; whereas systems rise out of individual exertions. Luthur was an individual. The very faults of an individual excite attention; he loses, but his cause (if good and he is powerful-minded) gains. This is the way of things; we promote truth through self-sacrifice . . .

So wrote the great conservative John Henry Newman. Newman knew that to be a true conservative is to be attacked as much by the extreme right as to be rebuffed by the left. He knew that conservatism is a kind of eternal balancing act, that to attempt to fit conservatism into a tight little system is to kill it. He knew that the principles of conservatism (in his case religious conservatism, but the point holds for political conservatism as well) must be firmly held, but not so tightly as to smother the life out of those principles. He knew, in short, what William F. Buckley has seemingly known since birth. It was the person of Bill Buckley who influenced me toward discovery of my own conservatism.

It was during my second year in college when, one evening, I happened to be watching a then-popular television interview show. Years later, in a letter to William F. Buckley, I recalled that chance viewing:

> . . . it was over ten years ago—close to twelve I suppose—that I saw you on the Mike Wallace "Nightbeat" show. It was an historic occasion for me, for your performance that night led me to investigate conservatism through *National Review*. In 1959 *National Review* accepted my first published article and ever since I've been depending on you and *National Review* for the most accurate, civilized, energetic, and entertaining presentation of the conservative point of view.
>
> . . . The funny part about it is that all I can remember of that "Nightbeat" interview was Wallace asking you "Are you saying that your church is the only true church?" and you (looking like David Frye at his best) grinning and saying "But, Mike, *of course* I believe it is the only true Church. If it were

not the only true Church why would I want to belong to it in the *first* place?" That isn't an exact quote but it comes close to what you said. I remember thinking "My *God*, I've always wanted to say that but I thought it would offend somebody!" From that moment on I was hooked.

. . . like most working-class kids who have intellectual pretensions, I discovered quite quickly that there were certain magazines one read, certain authors one quoted, certain jokes one made, certain attitudes one must have if one were to be taken seriously by professors. I need not tell you what those authors, magazines, etc. had in common—liberalism stalked the halls of Jersey City State College as well as the classes of Yale.

. . . I gather it is all but impossible for you to realize what agony it can be to be unsure and uncertain about what intellectual direction to take and to be unprepared to stand up to professors who, day by day, demonstrate that liberal attitudes are the only ones any self-respecting man would want to cultivate. I didn't know enough to combat them; I was half-convinced that they were correct; I was eager to assume the protective coloration of the young liberal, believing in what all good young liberals believe, embracing the gospel according to Norman Cousins or Jack Kennedy or whatever hero of the liberal left might be in favor. My God, it is difficult for a kid from my background to even begin to *know* that there is an intellectually respectable conservative position. The values of my family seemed to me to be correct—but how *could* they be when professors without Jersey City accents held them in open contempt (e.g., nothing is black or white, everything is gray; we must look at all things in a relative way, etc. etc. etc.).

Here is where you came in. Whatever else might be said about your accent it sure as hell has *never* been heard in Jersey City (or in Hoboken or Bayonne for that matter) and here you were, *openly* and unashamedly throwing your reactionary beliefs in the face of Mike Wallace! (John Henry Newman—a great man whose work I got to know relatively late in life—has said it all about the power of personality, of the "whole man" being the thinker, not just the brain . . . your presence on the show was proof of that). It was your attitude rather than your arguments—which I forgot—that impressed me so very much. Here was an honest-to-God intellectual who wasn't apologizing about his faith (*a la Commonweal*) and who really *enjoyed* arguing with liberals. I always got butterflies in the stomach when

> I tried to question a professor on some political or philosophical matter, and I began to think that the liberal had all the answers because the liberal answers were all there were.

Perhaps it takes a product of twelve years of Catholic schooling, old-style, to be able to recognize dogma when one sees it, but it was evident to me that what I was getting in most of my classes in college and in graduate school (University of Pennsylvania) was the secular equivalent of what I had been getting in only one class—religion—in Catholic high school and grammar school. Fighting against this indoctrination of dogmatic liberalism led me to investigate the intellectual roots of the traditional beliefs I had unquestioningly held.

Gradually, I began to question liberal dogma. With liberals, everything is open to question except, of course, liberalism. When the U-2 incident occurred, our history class assignment was to read and discuss an ad in the *New York Times,* a full-page *mea culpa* for snooping on our peace-loving Communist friends. We were expected to question U-2s, not those who denounce U-2s.

I began to neglect the liberal line of the classroom and to read on my own. And the more I read, the more I was convinced that the unexamined patriotism of my family, while un-chic in the eyes of intellectual sophisticates, was, upon reflection, based on a fundamental principle of conservatism; that my religion, to many liberals an authoritarian organization similar to Communism and fascism in its desire to chain minds, has in its moral teachings the bulwark of Western civilization; that the pride of my family in our Irish heritage was not vicious ethnocentrism to be hated or ridiculed, but a blessing to be praised. I discovered, in short, that I had been a kind of conservative without knowing it.

The kind of conservatism I speak of has for a long time been both unaware of itself and, naturally, unable to articulate its premises. The "instinctive," "visceral" conservatism of the urban "ethnic" Catholic is taken for granted. G. K. Chesterton's kind of conservatism had as its basis a belief in this instinctive conviction of the urban masses. It rests on a stable, structured social order.

What has happened, however, is that many of the children of "instinctive" conservatives have gone to school like good, upwardly mobile Americans. They have learned the arguments that hitherto had been the intellectual ammunition of educated liberals or of the minority of intellectuals who were conservative. Studs Lonigan's children didn't, I emphasize, *become* conservative (so much for the Argument from Social Science). They discovered through the process of study and debate that the life led by their parents had at its roots unarticulated but truthful principles which were either neglected or derided by college professors who were either consciously liberal or caught up in some fashionable left-liberal pose. The process by which this discovery occurs is worthy of being expanded upon because I believe it is happening more frequently today than ever before.

A few years ago, when I was teaching English in a suburban high school, I had a colleague named Joe. Joe taught high school sophomores in what is called an "honors" course. The brightest of the bright were allowed to take this course after undergoing careful screening to make certain only the best got in. It was a status symbol for two reasons: honors courses meant prestige in themselves and Joe was a gifted teacher. Having "had" Joe was an educational experience in itself.

Joe showed me his reading list for the course. It included works by Jean-Paul Sartre, Camus and Voltaire. I suggested that this might be a little bit much for fourteen- and fifteen-year-old children who weren't emotionally or intellectually prepared for, say, *No Exit* or *Candide*.

Wrong, Joe said. These kids have to be shaken up. They come to school with the prejudices of their homes and the church and they just don't *think*. It's our job as teachers to challenge them, to start them thinking.

"Thinking" meant to Joe adhering to certain skeptical and even cynical attitudes toward popularly held middle- and working-class beliefs. "Challenge" meant that he would do everything in his power to start a child "thinking" about, for example, the possibility of atheism. Once the child started ostensibly "thinking," presumably Joe's work was done. He had done his intellectual duty.

Although I'll admit it was a little odd in a high school situation, it is anything but odd if you take the educational world as a whole. There are millions of students who have been led to believe that there are two important things a person must do if he is to be intellectually respectable: the first is to have an "open mind" and the second is to "question" everything.

Students of irony will note that teachers who say this *never* say that one must question the absolute virtue of an open mind or have an open mind about questioning as an absolute virtue.

An open mind is usually held by this kind of liberal to be that state of the intellect which rejects all traditional morality and especially belief in a Supreme Being. "Questioning" is an exercise in methodological skepticism that seeks by unending debate to reduce to absurdity any belief in objective standards of morality or belief in a Supreme Being.

I was reminded of all this by the unleashing of the wolf packs on the college campuses in the late 60's. Where had all that hate come from?

Part of it came from the realization by many students that they had been "had." They were told at age fifteen the virtues of questioning, but no one ever told them *to question the worth of eternal questioning*. They knew that one was supposed to have an open mind, but they discovered that a consistently open mind could soon become functionally similar to a hole in the head.

Students want *truth*. It is as simple as that. They are no different from anyone else. Ultimately, they don't want charm or style. They don't want cute tricks. They want truth, and Joe and thousands of others like him have effectively demolished the concept of truth. Students can no longer believe in the beliefs of their parents and their churches—yet they are too bright to believe in the professors.

What has happened? Let's trace an urban conservative student's intellectual progress in today's higher education. It comes usually in two stages, the first occurring *before* he enters college.

Stage One: He is passive. He accepts views of parents and those who most closely affect his daily life—church, school, neighborhood associates. Usually this means an unexamined adherence to what might be called the *standard* emotional response to words such as: patriotism, God, law, right, wrong.

Stage Two: He is active. This stage usually is not reached until the person attends college or comes into contact—through magazines or books—with persons who question his responses to basic words. An example: a freshman will react to "patriotism" by equating it with simple, unexamined prejudices about the flag, Valley Forge, etc. A political science teacher will challenge that response by going through a process of argument leading to the conclusion that one can be loyal to one's nation by questioning it, by challenging popular concepts of patriotism, by sneering at such reactions as based upon "parent-Church" influences.

This second stage is quite complex and difficult to transcend. For most young Americans it is usually the introduction to what might be called non-prejudicial thought. The professors speak a different language; they do not accept the beliefs and values of the parents and the neighborhood. Indeed, they find those values and beliefs ludicrous, biased, bigoted, etc.

Now the student is faced with a dilemma; he discovers that reality is much more complicated than his parents and teachers told him; he knows he cannot get away with giving the usual stock responses in class because professors can immediately destroy them with incisive arguments based on what seems to be irrefutable evidence. Therefore, the student concludes that both the thinking methods and the beliefs of the two groups are somehow distinctly different.

If you believe in God, you must believe in God the way Uncle Louis does; Uncle Louis believes in a way that is uninformed, bigoted, not at all intellectually sophisticated and—therefore—not only his way of believing but the concepts he believes in must be erroneous.

The professor, on the other hand, usually believes in agnosticism in such a way that a freshman soon comes to admire not only his *method* (documentation, quotations, well-reasoned arguments) but its fruits, including agnosticism and cynicism about prejudices held by the working class.

So an urban conservative college student is confronted with what seems to him an insurmountable problem: if he continues to hold onto the *method* of his parents' beliefs, he cannot live with himself because he knows that such a method is intellectually disreputable. At the same time he cannot hold onto the content of their beliefs while his professors, day-in-and-day-out, demonstrate that if one thinks "intellectually," one arrives at certain conclusions about God (He isn't there), patriotism (it's a sham) and right and wrong (there are only shades of gray—except war; that is immoral).

This, I think, is why we see the allegedly irreversible shift from conservatism to a perverse form of liberalism among college students. Faced with what admittedly is the sophistication, breadth and depth of reading experience that professors have *vis-à-vis* students, a student would have to be superhuman to overcome the feeling that the ritualistic liberal professors are correct, not only in the *way* they think, *but in the conclusions they have reached.*

I, for one, cannot blame any student for reaching such a conclusion. The dogmatic assertions that pass for argument in an average family appear to a college student as vulgar, irrational and shameful when contrasted to the admirable exercises in logic, demonstration and irony that are characteristic of the best liberal professors.

What is wrong, of course, is *not* that the student has learned ways to challenge the beliefs of his parents. What *is* wrong is that he has *not learned how to use those same methods to challenge the beliefs of the professors who challenge his parents' beliefs.* No one on campus has ever said to him: "Yes, it is true your parents don't think in the sophisticated ways the professors do. But it does not therefore *logically* follow that the views held by your parents are undesirable and the views held by the professors are desirable. What matters is whether such views are true—and it is the conservative position that the traditional views *are,* for the most part, not only true, but demonstrably so. Take the idea of God, for example. You can believe in God the way Uncle Louis does or the way Bill Buckley does; it's the same God. But Buckley believes in Him after a rigorous analysis and thorough meditation. In this way, you might go on to the next stage.

Stage Three: Again, the student is active. He begins by *questioning the conclusions* of the professors; he questions their methods and their documentation. Ultimately, he questions the competence of even the most articulate men in areas of conduct and belief—all the while using the professors' very *own* thinking tools.

The student has then progressed from dogmatically-held prejudices, unexamined and half-understood, if at all, through the cynical but almost always convincing skepticism or leftist dogmatism of the professors to, finally, an intellectually-based, rationally-held position in line with the basic beliefs of his working-class parents—and of Western civilization at its height.

Viewed in this light, what passes for a liberal education in most colleges today should bring a blush to the cheek of even the most unabashed liberal or leftist professors.

Their argument has always been that they *must* present "the other side of the argument" because, after all, the students have received "the other side" from parents and church and school. It is, say the professors, only their intellectual duty to help shake these kids up, to have them "question" the values they bring to school.

But what about the "values" the students receive from the professors? Who will help shake up these kids about those ideas? Is it the professor's belief that his own values can be challenged *only* by methods and viewpoints of the working-class parents? If that were the case, the values held by the working class would, of course, be intellectually doomed. But that isn't the case at all. Throughout the major areas of modern thought, there is a responsible, scholarly, well-documented, rational, humane, intellectual position diametrically opposed to that of the relativists, liberal dogmatists and leftists. It is quite in line with the *conclusions*—if not the *methods* of argument—of parents, church, school . . . in short, of civilization.

Yet, where, oh, where can an urban conservative student hear this view on campus? He is constantly told that the battle is *only* between what he came to school with and what he is getting now. No one will tell him that there is another battle: that of questioning the stuff he is getting now without reverting solely to the kind of argumentation his parents "taught" him.

A conference of the University Centers for Rational Alternatives (September, 1973) featured a paper given by Professor W. Theodore de Bary of Columbia University, in which Professor de Bary suggested that at least part of acadême now recognizes the dangers of fostering a particularly critical outlook among students. According to *Measures,* UCRA's publication:

> Professor de Bary concluded with the challenging and controversial claim that general education must re-examine the primacy of the critical method among its value goals. This primacy has been supported, in Professor de Bary's view, by the university's perception of its students as persons growing out of a provincial and parochial dogmatism which called for the sophistication of skepticism and the methodology of critical intelligence . . .

In a perceptive article published in *Commentary* in June, 1972, Professor James Q. Wilson of Harvard wrote of the problems that arise from the kind of liberal intellectual approach that stresses criticism of accepted values:

> . . . Criticism is relentless and accepts no bounds; it may prosper when discourse is free and unconstrained but the price paid for that intellectual prosperity is the unceasing assault on those political and legal practices that have produced such freedom. And in the case of Herbert Marcuse, the critical faculty even comes to doubt the value of the freedom itself. Freedom exists because there first existed a certain kind of social order maintained and defined by laws, governments, and authority. Freedom cannot exist outside some system of order, yet no system of order is immune from intellectual assault.
>
> Intellectual criticism would have bounds if there were a widely-accepted principle of authority or theory of human nature on which certain political institutions could rest immune from eroding questions. At various times there have been, Jefferson believed, or wrote as if he believed, that political and civil liberty were among the natural rights of men. But the concept of "natural rights," I need hardly add, has been among

> the first principles to be criticized, for it implies by its use of the term "natural" that something exists beyond man's invention and thus beyond man's revision . . .

Wherever he turns, the urban conservative student finds liberalism in its many guises:

1. *The Liberal as Pop Humanist.* He/she appears on the late night talk shows either as a guest or a host. There is not a single intellectual, political, social or sexual perversion to the left of center about which he/she is not prepared to pour forth a deluge of understanding. If Attila the Hun, Jack the Ripper and the Mugger of the Year were all to appear on one of the talk shows, he/she would listen attentively to their tales and then say it all depended on how one looked at it. All of us aren't, after all, the *same* and who is to say just what is right. If some wretch who happens to be one degree to the right of the view of the editorial page of the *Washington Post* managed to get on such a show, the Pop humanist will spend the entire time clucking about Watergate, hunger in America and war crimes (American-style only). Pop humanism works only in one direction and its beneficiaries are usually spokesmen for dissent (dissension: any act of physical or verbal violence directed against conservative institutions or persons or against institutions or persons thought by dissenters to be conservative) or they are anti-social culture heroes out on parole. The Pop humanist liberal reads quite a bit and once even managed to browse through a book written by someone with a political philosophy slightly to the right of Arthur Schlesinger, Jr. The experience was harrowing and he/she now prefers to get news about conservatism from unbiased sources, e.g., Tom Wicker.

2. *The Liberal as Sage.* He wrote your political science textbook, has had eight of his books chosen as Book-of-the-Month selections, appears now and then to dispense tidbits of wisdom on television talk shows and is proud of the fact that a policeman bit him on the leg in Chicago in 1968. His articles appear regularly in *Harpers* and *Atlantic* and while he keeps slightly aloof from the *New York Review of Books* crowd (too much, really, that bunch) he wrote an article on the Meaning of Watergate for Homosexuals, published in that illustrious

journal. He is the American version of one of the Magi, except that if he were told to follow a star he would no doubt refuse because the Space program is *so* depressing to his humanist sensitivities. He has been saying the same things for thirty years (his message usually condenses to one word: More) and is paid handsomely for saying them. He keeps an icon of Adlai Stevenson hanging over his desk at Harvard and, when he dies, will have his ashes scattered over Hyde Park. When he was beaten up by drug-crazed graduate students during the late sixties, he blamed it all on the repressive tendencies of the Johnson Administration for inciting the kids to go beyond the limits of rational discourse. When the kids burned down his wing of the political science building with him in it, he contributed to the blaze by throwing in copies of *Profiles in Courage* to show his good faith.

3. *The Liberal as Media Zealot.* Sandy Van Wicker or Eric Lisagor, on television or in his newspaper column, has been fighting the good fight for years. An intimate of the best, i.e., richest, families on the left wing of the Democratic party, he is as much a celebrity as those he writes about or talks to on television. He was in Vietnam badgering young soldiers who were about to fly by helicopter to Cambodia, asking them if they were afraid (he didn't make that trip); he was in the middle of a prison riot, spewing forth compassion for the homosexual-rape artists and revolutionary strong-arm men who told him that they were being deprived of their rights; he has recently discovered white working-men but doesn't quite know what to make of them. He is confused because he knows they are all racists and reactionaries but, if the best people are to win, he is going to need these vermin—so what's a zealot to do? If there is a single social problem whose exploitation will help to cast scorn upon any politician to the right of Ramsey Clark, this guy will do an in-depth, i.e., two-minute report on the subject and, no matter what it is, he will open and close his report with a thirty-second shot of a starving black baby. He wept only once in his life—when it became clear that the Democratic party wouldn't nominate Gene McCarthy in 1968. But he looks forward to better days.

4. *The Liberal as Wine and Cheese Party Guru.* In the old days he was a cocktail party liberal guru but nobody worth knowing gives those anymore, so he has switched to wine and cheese bashes which are gauche but at least the wine is sometimes drinkable. He was the first person to say "re-order priorities" (at a party in Oswego, New York, in November, 1951) and is still saying it even though people are beginning to fall asleep when he opens his mouth. He was against the Vietnam War in 1938 and has a letter he wrote from prep school to prove it ("Dear Mom: When's the killing going to stop? Love, Charles"). He is open-minded to an alarming degree but only on one side of his head (left) and has trouble keeping his cheese down when someone mentions the flag. He hates American foreign policy since 1926 and can quote every revisionist historian down to the last misquotation. A kid was nice to him in 1969 and he has never forgotten it. When the conversation gets around to horror stories, he has one about the time a college English professor (later put away for his own good) asked his class to read one of Dos Passos' later novels, written after his disillusionment with the political left. He likes to refer to this as the incident that proved the stranglehold of the corporations on higher learning. He hates wine and cheese.

In high school the urban conservative probably was given a test similar to the one given in a suburban high school in 1972. Juniors at the school were given the test to help them find out what their political leanings were. The grading system for the test was as follows: 2 points for a "yes" or "agree" answer, 1 point for a "partly agree" answer and no points for a "no" or "disagree" answer. Anyone with a score of over 16 was defined as liberal. Here is the test:

POLITICAL VALUES UNIT

INTRODUCTION TO THE UNIT: This unit is designed to permit you to work by yourself and at your own speed. *Be sure to read all of the instructions very carefully as you work along. Not everyone will do the same things.*
PART I: ARE YOU A LIBERAL OR A CONSERVATIVE?
INSTRUCTIONS: Do you consider yourself a LIBERAL or a

CONSERVATIVE in politics? Are you even sure that you know what those two words mean? Below is a quick questionnaire that might help you in determining your political values. READ EACH QUESTION OR STATEMENT AND THEN CHECK THE RESPONSE YOU PREFER BEST:

YES	NO	
____________	____________	1. In general, do you think the federal government in Washington should make sure that every American has a good job, a good income, and a good life?
____________	____________	2. Do you favor the federal government giving financial aid to public schools?
____________	____________	3. Do you favor the federal government giving financial aid to private schools?
____________	____________	4. Do you favor the federal government providing a health insurance program for elderly people?
____________	____________	5. Do you favor the federal government providing programs to train and hire poor people in the cities?
____________	____________	6. Do you favor the federal government giving money to low income families to help pay their rent?
____________	____________	7. Do you favor a federal law that says that you must sell your home to anyone who can afford it regardless of their race or religion?
____________	____________	8. Do you favor a law that would keep Negroes from serving on court juries?

________	________	9. Do you favor a law that would prevent employers and labor unions from discriminating against Negroes?
________	________	10. Do you favor giving money to neutral countries that refuse to support American foreign policy unless they agree with it?

AGREE	PARTLY AGREE	DISAGREE	
_____	________	________	11. The federal government should provide for the basic needs of the people.
_____	________	________	12. The federal government should control the prices set by private industry.
_____	________	________	13. The federal government should spend more money at home and overseas even if it has to borrow the money to do it.
_____	________	________	14. The federal government should make sure Negroes have the right to vote.
_____	________	________	15. It should make no difference where immigrants come from.
_____	________	________	16. Demonstrations against our Vietnam policy should be permitted.

It is immediately obvious that most of the questions are, of course, not those that can be answered by "yes" or "no" or be regarded as representative of "liberal" or "conservative" views, but the fact that questions 14 to 16 could be judged by a high school teacher as ones that can be answered in either a liberal or a conservative way is staggering. But, if a high school junior feels it makes no difference where immigrants come from or that Negroes should have the right to vote or that demonstrations should be permitted, he discovers he is a liberal and also learns that to think otherwise is to think as a conservative. No wonder he wants to be thought of as liberal.

Where, then, is the intelligent young urban conservative going to be able to discover his own conservatism? He's going to have to do it on his own. He is going to have to listen and read and think and make a lot of mistakes. He is going to have to realize that the kind of intellectual position he knows is right for him is simply not going to be given a fair presentation in the majority of American schools. There is no plot or conspiracy about this. It simply reflects the fact of the unchanged dominance of liberal philosophy in American education. Why this particular philosophy is dominant is a question that would demand—and deserve—another book. The relevant fact here is that it *is* dominant and that the urban conservative is going to have to resort to outside reading.

I asked two conservatives who share with me in varying degrees the street corner conservative viewpoint to list the conservative books that had helped them to understand their own conservatism. The answer of Patrick J. Buchanan, former Special Assistant to former President Nixon, shows that for many conservatives the "intellectual" discovery came after the college years:

> Frankly, I didn't read conservative books in college; I read generally what was on the curriculum, plus outside reading recommended by the professors. And conservatism, I think, came less from books than from up-bringing . . . One book I thought impressive when I first read it was Burnham's "Suicide of the West;" . . . Personal convictions about the character of man and society . . . were what led (me) to the books to find the philosophical under-pinnings for what was in the gut . . .

Here is Pat Buchanan's list of books, on the basis of his own experience, that might be of help to the urban conservative student: George Orwell, *Animal Farm*; *Homage to Catalonia*; *1984*; Eric Hoffer, *The True Believer*; *The Temper of Our Time*; *The Ordeal of Change*; Malcolm Muggeridge, *Jesus Rediscovered*; C. S. Lewis, *The Screwtape Letters*; Arthur Koestler, *Darkness at Noon*; Walter Lippmann, *The Public Philosophy*; D. W. Brogan, *The American Character*, *The Price of Revolution;* John W. Aldridge, *The Country of the Young;* John Coyne, *The Kumquat Statement*; Duncan Williams, *Trousered Apes*; (The Rev.) Andrew Greeley, *Why Can't They Be Like Us;* Edward Banfield, *The Unheavenly City*; Whittaker Chambers, *Cold Friday*; Tom Wolfe, *Mau-Mauing the Flak Catcher*; Arnold Beichman, *Nine Lies About America*; Stanley Loomis, *Paris in the Terror*; Richard Weaver, *The Southern Tradition at Bay*; Jonathan Swift, *Gulliver's Travels*; Ernest Hemingway, *The Sun Also Rises*.

Richard Whalen, author of *The Founding Father* and *Catch the Falling Flag*, provided this list: Alexander Hamilton, James Madison and John Jay, *The Federalist Papers*; Henry Thoreau's *Walden* and *Essays*; Alexis de Tocqueville's *Democracy in America*; F. A. Hayek's *Constitution of Liberty* and *Road to Serfdom*; Arthur Koestler's *Darkness at Noon*; André Malraux's *Man's Fate* and (of course) . . . *all* of George Orwell—especially *Down and Out in Paris & London* and *The Road to Wigan Pier*.

He adds: "Orwell, it seems to me, has special appeal to the working class youth in search of a politics to sustain the values he cherishes. Orwell's 'socialism' is not very different from our own creed, when you boil away the rhetoric."

My own list would certainly include those books mentioned by Buchanan and Whalen, with the addition of anything by John Henry Newman, G. K. Chesterton, H. L. Mencken, C. S. Lewis and Bill Buckley. Anyone looking for insight into the "libertarian" side of conservatism must read Ludwig von Mises' huge, often difficult, sometimes cranky masterpiece *Human Action*. A street corner conservative will not agree with all of Von Mises, but can learn much from him about economic common sense.

But the differences between "libertarian" and "traditional" conservatives' approaches are beyond the scope of this book. It is enough to say that Pat Buchanan and Dick Whalen have shown that a young conservative, searching for the values of his own past in philosophy and literature, must not confine himself to some "Approved List of Conservative Authors." George Orwell's approach to socialism is not only intellectually admirable but can serve as a model for a conservative's approach to his own political or philosophical beliefs.

At any rate, three points must be made concerning the difficulties facing any young urban conservative seeking to find his way out of the liberal maze:

1. It won't be easy. You'll probably have to do most of the work yourself. At first you'll lose more arguments than you win. But remember: the other guys may at first know more than you do, but they'll never know better.

2. Conservatism isn't a *thing*. It's a kind of inclination of the spirit. There are no rules. Traditionalists can (must!) learn from libertarians. There will be arguments with those who also call themselves conservatives but who disagree with you on important matters. In these cases remember the ancient formula for arguing: On those things about which we disagree, freedom. On those things about which we agree, unity. In all things, love.

3. Either you have a philosophy or you don't. If you don't, you simply go from one problem to another, sometimes stumbling on to right answers, sometimes blundering into disasters. This is popularly called "pragmatism" and is praised by those who either don't know what William James wrote or don't care. If you do have a philosophy, it behooves you to find out as much about it as possible. In order to do this, you are going to have to read. A lot. You are going to have to argue. A lot. You are going to have to take old beliefs, tear them apart, reassemble them . . . you are going to have a hell of a good time. I've been there. But, still, I envy you.

Chapter 4
Looking for the Invisible Man

> When you come to the normal working class the position is totally different. To begin with, there is no short-cut into their midst . . . The middle-class Socialist enthuses over the proletariat and runs 'summer-schools' where the proletarian and the repentant bourgeois are supposed to fall upon one another's necks and be brothers forever; and the bourgeois visitors come away saying how wonderful and inspiring it has all been (the proletarian ones come away saying something different) . . .
>
> —George Orwell
> *The Road to Wigan Pier*, 1937

A few years ago a woman from California wrote one of those songs that just happens to catch on. It became a commercial success, was listened to and talked about for a while and then died a natural death from over-exposure. The song told us of "ticky-tacky" houses inhabited by "ticky-tacky" people. The message was clear: we live in a nation which is being smothered by conformity. Our conformist suburban "ticky-tacky" housing developments, it seemed, reflect the personalities of their robot-like inhabitants and the conformist spirit of the nation.

It so happened that, at the time, I was working during college summer vacation as a meter-reader for a gas and electric company in Jersey City. My job took me to many types of dwellings, from six-family walk-ups to enormous housing developments and the more homes I saw, the more I became convinced that the song was wrong. The housing developments may have looked alike from the outside, but the inside of each development home was different, reflecting the particular taste or, if you wanted to get nasty about it, lack of taste of the owner. Far from being proof of conformity, the mass-produced homes of the developments were proof of the incredible diversity of American life. Yet, day after day I would hear that song and, what was worse, would listen to people tell me how accurate the song was in exposing the outrageous conformity of our national life.

If I had not had the opportunity as a meter-reader to see the reality of the housing-development, I would perhaps have gone along, willy-nilly, with the intellectual attitude represented by the song. At that time the "conformity" thesis was a fashionable idea without which no cocktail party conversation could be a success. The intellectuals who try to shape our opinions told us we were conformists and what could be better proof of our conformity than our mass-produced homes, each indistinguishable from the other? The only thing wrong with that idea was that it wasn't true and it was most demonstrably untrue precisely where the intellectuals told us it was most true, i.e., in the Levittowns and other developments. If you simply went to the developments and looked at the obviously identical houses, you couldn't help but notice that each house was also different because the people who lived in the houses were different.

When I raised this point with my liberal friends, I was inevitably told that no matter what I had seen with my own eyes, no matter how much evidence of diversity I saw every day as a meter-reader, no matter how much evidence piled up to disprove the fashionable doctrine—the doctrine was right. Americans were conformists, proof of it was in our mass-produced housing and, by God, let's have an end to quibbling! Were there not dozens, even scores of books laboriously fashioned by professors and other holy men which *proved* we were conformists?

The "ticky-tacky" song craze finally ended, but the intellectual malady it represented lingers on. The gap between the fashionable ideas of the intellectual and the realities of American life has, if anything, widened, nowhere more strikingly than in the case of urban conservatives.

Those same intellectuals, who for years had complained that they were not being listened to by politicians, were finally listened to in the nineteen-sixties. The cities, we were told, would become utopian playgrounds of health, happiness and brotherhood under the new liberal intellectual dispensation. The result, after an expenditure of tens of billions of tax-payers' dollars on Great Society programs, was reported in a *New York Times* article on May 25, 1972. The headline told the story: ***An Epitaph for the Great Society:***

> . . . a distinguished group of Brookings Institute economists, including some of the Johnson Administration's social engineers, have pronounced, reluctantly but manfully, a more formal epitaph for the Great Society.
>
> In a brilliant, book-length analysis of national priorities, issued today, they conclude that the multiplication of dollars and programs brought not solutions for such problems as welfare reform, day care and city finance but a multiplication of dilemmas. And now the dilemmas threaten to become paralyzing.
>
> . . . In the last 10 years, the Federal Government has been called on increasingly to do things it does not know how to do . . .

Those not yet used to liberal intellectual double-think might find the *New York Times* piece a bit puzzling. After all, was it not the same intellectuals, now damning the Great Society programs, who, only a few years ago, were telling us the Great Society was, well, great? In order to understand how liberals can, (a) get credit for the creation of dynamic new programs, (b) manage to disappear when the programs explode and, (c) write scholarly articles disclosing why it was inevitable that the programs should have failed, thereby getting credit for a "brilliant, book-length" analysis, it is necessary to understand the Law of the Liberal Double-Effect. This law states that any federally-funded program created and managed by liberals is good until the liberals declare it to be bad. When it is good the liberals gain credit for its goodness; when it is found to be bad, the liberals gain credit for discovering its badness.

To the man on the street corner, the "brilliant" report of the liberal intellectuals, documenting their own failures while at the same time somehow or other looking noble and wise for making the discovery of the fiasco of the Great Society, was simply another example of their intellectual arrogance and ignorance with which he has had to live as long as he can remember.

Whether the liberal is abusing him for living in mass-produced homes (which are better than the flats he was living in, can be afforded by the average working man and are the only alternatives he had to living in neighborhoods made unlivable because of the predictable results of liberal theories about guilt, morality and the causes of crime) or scolding him for supporting four Presidents in the Vietnam War (a war the liberals' "best and brightest," i.e., not too good and not too bright, in David Halberstam's phrase, goofed), the man on the street corner has long been the victim and the target of the intellectual élite. Today, however, the urban conservative is threatened by something far more dangerous to his welfare: liberal attempts at beneficence. In order to understand why these attempts to cuddle-up are dangerous, consider the following:

In the 1960's, after the liberals had taken credit for "thoughtful" anti-Communism (see 1961 liberal praise of JFK Inaugural speech) and supported American intervention in Vietnam, they decided it was all wrong (see current liberal scorn for JFK's Inaugural speech) and started criticizing what they themselves had done. The Law of the Liberal Double-Effect held them blameless, whether they were initiating a war action or criticizing the action they initiated. At any rate, there evolved a specific, left-liberal criticism directed against our efforts in Vietnam. This criticism stated that the United States simply did not understand the nature of society in Vietnam and, therefore, was unable to cope with problems that had their roots deep in Vietnamese history and tradition. In 1972, one of the publishing hits of the season was *Fire in the Lake* by Frances Fitzgerald, a book whose major thesis was precisely this: America "utterly misinterpreted the reality of the country," according to the book's jacket blurb, "and the Vietnamese and Americans failed to comprehend each other's acts, motives and even words."[13]

The Vietnam War is super-abundant in ironies, both tragic and comic, and here we come upon yet another. The very same left-liberals who castigated the United States government for not understanding a faraway people and their customs are now engaged in a misunderstanding of their own, in this country. Having recently discovered or, to give some of them their due, re-discovered the urban conservative, the left-liberal intellectual is doing exactly what he accuses the government of doing in Vietnam—utterly misunderstanding the reality of the neighborhoods. Using every concept from vulgar Marxism to Social Science Solemnity, the intellectuals have invaded the neighborhoods. Their efforts to pacify voters who went the wrong way, i.e., for conservative candidates, are meeting with less success than the American efforts toward pacification did in Vietnam.

Indeed, there are striking similarities between the American effort in Vietnam and the intellectual efforts in the urban neighborhoods. Both seek to contain the enemy (communism, to the U.S.; conservatism, to the intellectuals); both rely on money and technological expertise (weaponry for the U.S.; "studies" and federally-funded "programs" for the liberals); both have difficulty understanding basic concepts of the

13. *Fire in the Lake,* Frances Fitzgerald, Atlantic, Little, Brown. The entire book illustrates the thesis of American misunderstanding, but Chapter One, "States of Mind," and much of Chapter Three, "Sovereign of Discord," are of particular interest.

people with whom they are dealing. How many American advisors could give an intelligent summary of Confucianism? How many liberal intellectuals could give an intelligent and sympathetic account of Roman Catholicism as it is practiced among urban conservatives?

The Vietnamese simply didn't fit some of the concepts we had ready for them. The urban conservative doesn't fit the concept of "ethnic-working-class-union-member-middle-American." He is all of these things but he is also something else, something that is at the heart of what the sociologists call his "life-style." If he is seen simply as Economic Man, then all that would have to be done to bring him back to the Democratic party would be to focus the changes on the economic issue.

Yet the average urban conservative wonders who these people are and why they are saying these nice things about him. For years he was ignored by them except when it came time to vote for liberal politicians. Now that the urban conservative has begun to show signs of independence, he is being wooed, rather clumsily, by those who only a short while ago were calling him a racist, a conformist, a dullard and a reactionary. He was, after all, to blame for the horrors of the slave trade, the plantation and the lynching bee—or so said his liberal intellectual "betters."

That these horrors took place when the ancestors of the urban conservatives were behind a plow in Poland or digging potatoes in Ireland did not matter to the media, academic and political élites. Somebody, after all, was to blame and it must be that guy watching television with the can of beer in his hand. Eventually, the guy crushed the beer can with one hand and started shouting back at his accusers.

If the Democratic liberal establishmentarians had bothered to listen to the urban conservative before he turned against them, they might have heard something like this:

> I am an invisible man. No, I am not a spook like those who haunted Edgar Allan Poe; nor am I one of your Hollywood-movie ectoplasms. I am a man of substance, of flesh and bone, fiber and liquids—and I might even be said to possess a mind. I am invisi-

> ble, understand, simply because people refuse to see me. Like the bodiless heads you see sometimes in circus side-shows, it is as though I have been surrounded by mirrors of hard, distorting glass. When they approach me they see only my surroundings, themselves, or figments of their imagination—indeed, everything and anything except me.

These are the opening words of Ralph Ellison's memorable novel, *Invisible Man,* spoken by a Negro; the same words could have been spoken by urban conservatives in the nineteen-sixties. Scorned by the intellectual, ignored by the mass media, derided for his patriotism, blamed for racial injustice, ridiculed for his moral values, forgotten by the opinion-makers and taken for granted by government, the urban conservative was, for a long time, the new invisible man and, like the black American, he didn't like it.

In the Orwellian sense, he might have been called more invisible than others. Nobody, to paraphrase a title of a book by another black writer, James Baldwin, knew his name. To some he was the "blue-collar worker"; to others, the "ethnic American"; to still others, "the middle-American"—he simply hadn't been important enough to label. His children were usually not considered when "youth" was talked about. He was fair game for Italian or Polish "jokes," which, if told about a Negro or Jew, would have brought down the wrath of the establishmentarian gods. Fascist, pig, bigot, racist, know-nothing, authoritarian—these were the names that were thrown in his face for ten years. He was invisible because government and the media and the intellectuals who shape our national vision refused to see him.

In their deepest sense, the problems of the urban conservative were spiritual. As a Roman Catholic, which most were, he had seen tremendous, seemingly inexplicable, changes take place in the liturgy. He accepted them because the Church wanted it that way, but he resented it, too.

Nobody asked *him* if the Mass should be said in English. Nobody asked him if he liked guitars; nobody asked him if he liked to hear the music of Simon and Garfunckel while he was receiving the body and blood of Christ. Nobody in the media asked him about the complexities of integration, and he was subjected to the often subtle, sometimes blunt but always present, abuse of the nightly news show pundits who live in lily-white, upper-income neighborhoods themselves. Nobody asked his kids what they thought of the Vietnam War—or, if the kids did say they supported the President, they were ignored or used as bad examples. Nobody cared about the invisible man except his family.

Nobody wrote compassionate novels about *him.* Nobody hired him when it came time to have a minority viewpoint on television. David Brinkley's eyebrows did not eloquently protest when the white worker was given a raw deal.

So he sat there, on Saturday night, looking at a television world he never made, hearing his kids mouth the jargon of bums and hippies, knowing that tomorrow he would hear the priest deliver a sermon on how badly he (the conservative, not the priest) had treated the black man for the past four hundred years. He sat there realizing that his son was dissatisfied with working as a meter-reader or in the factory where he himself had worked for thirty years . . . he sat there and drank his beer and brooded.

He had much to brood about, perhaps too much for anyone to handle. He didn't want to become a fad, a hula hoop of social concern. He simply wanted to be taken seriously, for his faith in God is the faith of the fathers and his love of country is the love of the founders and his desire to see his family gain opportunities he never had is the desire that built America . . . but no one seemed to care. He probably didn't read the *New Yorker*, except in his dentist's waiting-room, but if he had, he would have found, in the most establishmentarian liberal magazine, an attack on his religion unlike any made in a reputable magazine in recent history.

Yet, when James Baldwin wrote, in *Letter from a Region in My Mind* (1963), that "the real architect of the Christian Church was not the disreputable, sunbaked Hebrew who gave it his (sic) name but the mercilessly fanatical and self-righteous St. Paul," and "in the realm of power, Christianity has operated with an unmitigated arrogance and cruelty," and that the principles of the Christian Church are "Blindness, Loneliness and Terror"—not a single liberal voice was raised against the historical distortion, the lies and the fanaticism of Baldwin. Liberal intellectuals whose vocation imposed upon them the obligation to make intellectual distinctions not only allowed Baldwin and his numerous imitators to say the most outrageous nonsense about Christianity without criticism, but applauded them for saying it. And the urban conservative, to whom the Church was like a mother, wondered why.

At the same time, Father Groppi, in the name of a Higher Christianity, i.e., one known only to him and his demonstrators, led his marches for integration through the neighborhoods of the ethnics and urban conservatives. The media cheered, while noting with grave disapproval the fact that some of the urban conservatives had acted rather rudely toward the marchers. What right, after all, did the urban conservatives have to behave in such a manner? They were guilty. James Baldwin had said so—in the pages of the *New Yorker*, between perfume ads—and James Baldwin was, of course, sensitive and, most important, black.

And there it was. Black. Race. Racism. Once more the Law of the Liberal Double-Effect was working. The liberals, who had total federal power for over thirty years, who ran the television networks where no black man or woman was ever seen, who ran most major newspapers that had no black reporters, who ran the government in which no black man ever held a top position, whose personal experience with integrated housing was the family mansion where the servants lived-in . . . these same liberals now were taking credit for discovering the plight of the black man.

With "we-are-all-guilty" editorials and self-lacerating cocktail party chatter they snuggled up to guilt for a while, enjoying the indescribable pleasures of the fashionable penitent: Look, darling, my new sackcloth-and-ashes just came! But this thrill, like so many others they had become used to, began to wear off and another target of guilt was needed: America itself and particularly the racists that helped build it, those who lived in the urban neighborhoods or who had just moved or, to use the leftist term, "fled" to the suburbs where, for the first time in their lives, they had a chance to live among grass and trees and open space. They were the guilty ones. They used words like "nigger" and "coon." "White-working-class-animosity" became the whipping boy for the result of hundreds of years of complex historical and social situations.

Then, slowly, gradually but unmistakably, something began to happen.

Politically, it centered around George Wallace. His amazing primary record in 1964 dumbfounded the liberals. Of course it was, in one sense, to be expected—Wallace was a racist and the rednecks and oafs in the northern states who had voted for him were racists, everyone knew that. But still . . . the white worker had always known his place, had tipped his hat to his liberal "betters" in politics and the academy and was grateful for a pat on the head or a scratch behind the ear after being dealt a few kicks. How could he *do* anything like this to people who had been kind to him?

Although the media wanted to believe that racism was at the heart of the discontent of the urban conservatives, there was more to it than that. In his *The Making of the President 1968,*[14] Theodore H. White wrote this about young Wallace supporters:

> Now, here in September was yet another alienated group—the young working people of the industrial cities. They had seen the students, the middle-class young, their social "betters" rioting and blood-letting on television. Now they were being given a cause of their own. They had lived in the industrial cities ignored, unheard, unlistened to, their problems and aches unacknowledged by government or media; they had listened to learned commentators and found few spokesmen for what bothered them. Now they listened to George Wallace, because no one else seemed to speak their language . . .

During the 1968 Presidential campaign I flew on the Nixon plane as a speechwriter. On every trip a different group of the traveling national press flew on the same plane. I do not remember ever seeing one black face in this group. But from

14. *The Making of the President 1968*, Theodore H. White, p. 350.

time to time, almost all of them reminded their colleagues that the Nixon rallies did not have too many black faces in the crowd. They never looked at each other. So intent were the liberal reporters upon discrediting Conservatives or Republicans or white workers that they never bothered to look at their own ranks where, if integration were to come at all, black faces should have been seen more and more frequently by 1968.

When Richard Nixon was elected President, the rumbling grew even louder. The ominous, sullen silence of the white neighborhoods was being filled with angry cries, not of despair or bitterness, but of rage—rage against the liberals who had for so long used the urban conservatives as whipping boys. Now the liberals were gone from power. Now was a time for conservatives to get attention from someone who understood what they were talking about. There was rebellion going on and it was directed against the élites of government and media and university.

Joseph Kraft, nationally syndicated columnist, wrote:

> Social tension in the United States, being a subject usually studied by the educated, is generally blamed on the less educated. But every day announces that a main source of trouble is an overconfident attitude of snobbish contempt on the part of the American elite . . .

Richard Harwood of the *Washington Post* wrote of "the uneasy Dayton housewife," the prototype of the American voter in 1970 as seen by Richard Scammon and Ben Wattenberg in their *The Real Majority:*

> There is both promise and danger in this situation. If the progressive and compassionate figures in the political life of the 1970's turn their backs on the problems of the Dayton housewife, if they equate her concerns with "bigotry" and "racism," they will not only suffer at the polls; they will leave the field to the Wallaceites and bring on, to one degree or another, the repression no rational man can desire.

He also wrote of the alienation of working-class youth and quoted Sen. Edward Kennedy:

We simply cannot allow a love affair with campus youth on the issue of war to weaken or obscure the close tie the party has always had with the labor movement and the working man.

Bruce Biossat wrote:

Until fairly recently only a few key Democrats (like National Chairman Lawrence O'Brien) have appeared to grasp what is happening. Now, with the exception of some rather ardent liberal types like John Kenneth Galbraith, the older party, too, is waking up.

By now, with a host of blue-collar worker studies and reports, everybody knows what's eating at these people. They see the blacks as threatening, they detest students who disrupt colleges they themselves never got to but want their own children to attend; they are hanging on to the lower rungs of affluence by the weakest of grips.[15]

The "hard-hat" demonstrations against the peaceniks and in favor of President Nixon in 1970, suddenly and dramatically, brought the new invisible man a degree of recognition from the liberal establishment. Andrew Greeley, writing in the *New Republic*, warned its readers that they should have paid attention to the white working class because: "However virtuous the present radical movement may be, it has turned off somewhere between 60 and 90 percent of the American people."

Jimmy Breslin, writing of construction workers in *New York* magazine, said:

the day somebody can get to the Primo Riccis and talk to them and at least get them wavering on the war, have them stay by their trucks instead of parading for Nixon, that is the day you can stop worrying about generals planning to send young men into Cambodia or Laos. And show me the afternoon when there is a parade in New York and one of the signs says, "Primo Wants the War to End," show me that day and I'll show you troops out of Vietnam by nightfall.

In other words, it is good anti-war politics to pay attention to those slobs who, for all their blatant patriotism and flag-

15. All quotations were written within two weeks during July-August, 1970.

waving, can be of use to the liberals and the left and anybody with a grudge against Nixon.

There is evident callousness and cynicism in a viewpoint that sees the urban conservative as important enough to be exploited for propaganda purposes, but not important enough to have his own hawkish views on the war given consideration. What is not so evident is the underlying assumption that his view on the war or morality or social justice or anything but the fate of the Mets is, by the very fact that it is his, beneath consideration by liberal writers and intellectuals. It is this assumption that has been identified by some liberals as one of the major causes of the alleged alienation of the urban conservative, an alienation deeper and more dangerous in its potential for domestic trouble in the United States than the more publicized alienation of the young and the black. Michael Novak, a liberal Catholic theologian and a Sargent Shriver speechwriter who blasted his fellow liberals for their "reverse-twist racism," wrote that the whites of the lower-middle-class might erupt in "an apocalyptic rage that will make student riots seem like sorority teas."

All of this reached a climax in 1972. The invisible man had become visible once more and had the opportunity to watch George McGovern of South Dakota make goo-goo eyes at him. Sociologists began to appear from nowhere, tape recorders in hand, to find out what the street corner guy was doing. He was, we all discovered, an "ethnic."

Ethnicity, blue-collarism and middle-Americanism became the hot number during the late sixties and early seventies campaigns. Politicians who would ordinarily faint from culture shock if a real worker ever attended one of their dinner parties suddenly became friends of the common man. This trend reached its outer limits when Sargent Shriver, of the Maryland Shrivers, was seen on television quaffing beer with a neighborhood workman.[16] Good old Sarge, the one candidate to have when you're having more than one. Even the *Nation*, which in the good old days used to print anti-Catholic articles

16. There is no truth to the rumor that, when confronted with a beer, Shriver demanded to know the vintage year.

by Paul Blanchard, discovered the blue-collar virtues. The *New Republic*, that bastion of establishmentarian liberal virtues, published articles about the "blue–ing" of America.

This new liberal discovery of the urban conservative as an "ethnic" is, I believe, as dangerous to him in the long run as it is gratifying in the short. After years of neglect he is being noticed by liberal politicians, the media, scholars and by almost anyone who can make use of him as raw material. Are you a politician? Get the ethnic vote! Are you a media type? Do something about ethnics, it sells! Are you a sociology student? Find a tape recorder, get some Hungarian truckdriver blowsy with a six-pack, turn on the old machine and you have yourself an instant master's thesis!

But the limits of ethnicity are, well, ethnic. The politicians' ritualistic election-year praise of the virtues of goulash pleases goulash-loving voters, and when they are pleased the politician is pleased. Yet, what does it all lead to, this biennial and quadrennial rediscovery of exotic foods and folk-dances? The paths of ethnic discovery and exploitation lead but to the voting booth. It is strictly an election year phenomenon and, as such, can be turned on and off by those who need the ethnic's vote or his story.

To praise someone merely because his grandfather came from Minsk or County Mayo is to create a kind of "election-year-only" universe in which a politician pays attention only so far as a clearly discernible cause-and-effect relationship can be seen to exist between his need for a vote and the ethnic's ability to meet that need. The urban conservatives are not only "ethnics," they are heirs to one of the greatest intellectual and moral traditions the world has ever known. It is in their interest to break out of the "ethnic" stereotype imposed on them by politicians and the media, a stereotype as damaging to them in its own way as were the bigoted stereotypes that greeted their ancestors when they came to America. They should demand to be dealt with as human beings, not simply as sociological data made incarnate. In short, now that the urban conservative at last has the establishment's attention, it is in his interest to state that his social, political, philosophical, ethical and metaphysical concerns count as much as, even more than, the fact of his father's birthplace.

Some old-style Democratic liberal intellectuals, usually but not exclusively, those who knew George McGovern's 1972 presidential candidacy was a disaster area from the start, still cling to the myth of working-class solidarity. But they recognize that the worker has gotten the message from the new-style Democratic intellectual hierarchy over the years and that he has done precisely what the new-style Democratic intellectuals logically should have wanted him to do, i.e., turn his back on them and go looking for another party. These old-style liberals are even now trying to pick up the pieces, but they have a difficult, if not impossible, job to do because, to judge by their best and brightest, they do not yet fully recognize what has happened and why.

In 1972, Jack Newfeld and Jeff Greenfield wrote *A Populist Manifesto* which was called by Senator Edward Kennedy "a program for the millions of ordinary men and women who believe that government ought to serve the people, not just the special interests." The authors were shrewd enough to know that liberalism had been universally discredited and—without acknowledging that they once supported the politicians, backed the programs and shared the attitude they now deplore—they donned the blue collar, discovered the joys of ethnicity, and wrote about the poor working man as if they had always been a pal of the guy who sends his kid to Holy Redeemer School, who bowls on Thursday nights and who, when he thinks of it at all, hates the kind of cynical bidding for his favor illustrated by *A Populist Manifesto.*

Newfeld had gained some notoriety by his discovery that Bobby Kennedy was an "existentialist politician," which discovery would come as a shock to Gabriel Marcel or Jean-Paul Sartre but which pleased many liberals who wanted Bobby to be something other than JFK's hatchet-man and the former aide to Senator Joseph McCarthy. Greenfield's view of the working man might be better understood in light of a passage he wrote for Jerry Bruno in *The Advance Man.* The voice in the following passage is the voice of Bruno but the thought is typical of liberals trying to recapture that first, fine careless rapture of blue-collar affection:

> In New York City, Lindsay is poison in blue-collar areas; and the anti-Lindsay quality of many of the hardhat demonstrations have probably communicated themselves out to other parts of the country. What can Lindsay do? The same thing John Kennedy did with the Protestant ministers. He has to go right into those factories, and to those construction sites, and talk it out. It's entirely possible that by '72 the economy will have wiped out the resentment about Lindsay being too kind to blacks and kids. I watch these hardhats bragging about their patriotism, but when was the last time they didn't strike a missile plant or defense site when the issue was money? No, I think money is the key issue, and if we still have a recession-inflation, or if we have a depression by '72, they'll turn off a lot of that anti-Lindsay stuff.

In short, what this country needs is John Lindsay, and if it takes a depression to get the blue-collars to vote for Lindsay, so be it. There has not been such a display of blatant contempt for ordinary people since the days of Jay Gould. It is not necessary to add that John Lindsay did not turn on the blue-collars in the primary campaigns of 1972 and faded into show business on a regular basis.[17]

The Rise of the Unmeltable Ethnics by Michael Novak was the most ambitious liberal attempt to bring those wandering ethnics back to the fold. Novak's credentials are impeccable: he is an intellectual, a liberal and an ethnic.

His book is an excellent guide to liberal intellectual follies. It is amply documented and contains innumerable insights into the ethnic mind. It is an invaluable survey of intellectual fads and biases. Indeed, it is altogether a book of which Novak can justly be proud. There is only one thing wrong with it. It takes quite valid premises and arrives at quite erroneous conclusions.

17. Both Greenfield and Bruno worked in the successful 1974 gubernatorial campaign of Hugh Carey. Carey's contribution to political philosophy was to lose 30 pounds, get his hair cut short and hire David Garth to sell him on television like a winner of the Slenderella Sweepstakes. It worked. This strange marriage of political pragmatism and No-cal is being touted as the new thing in liberal circles . . . could be.

Novak correctly diagnoses the disease afflicting the ethnics as galloping liberalism in the downhill phase. Yet his cure for liberalism is . . . liberalism. He writes that his experience as a speechwriter for Sargent Shriver convinced him "that many people were hungry for a new politics." To assuage that hunger, Novak seeks a different kind of liberalism, ". . . not wedded to universal Reason . . . and whose base lies rather in the imagination and in the diversity of human stories." Here, of course, the question arises whether anyone could ever be so intellectually or politically hungry that the ideas of Sargent Shriver would be welcomed as food unless, of course, in true liberal tradition, there is a resort to forced-feeding. ("Open wide, we know what's good for you.")

Novak states that he long co-existed with liberal intellectuals who had nothing but scorn for the kind of people with whom he was raised. He writes:

> I never intended to think this way. I never intended to begin writing—ye gods!—as an *ethnic*. I never intended to dig up old memories.
>
> What began to prod me were political events. The anomaly in American publishing and television of William F. Buckley, Jr., had long troubled me: a Catholic who was making a much-needed criticism of American "enlightenment," but from a curiously Anglo-Saxon and conservative point of view. I hoped he was not a dotted line which a larger Catholic movement would fill in.

What immediately captures the attention of a conservative upon reading that passage is Novak's use of the word "anomaly" to describe the appearance of William F. Buckley in publishing and on television. This "troubles" Novak—but for the wrong reason. He, a liberal, is not troubled, as he should be, because the appearance of a conservative in the liberal-dominated media world is so rare as to be seen as an anomaly, but only because Buckley is successful. In one sense, of course, it is perfectly understandable why he should not be upset about this. A liberal intellectual in the United States accepts as the natural order of things the exclusion of conservatives from the theoretically free marketplace of ideas. Yet, Novak is obviously not just another liberal intellectual, but a serious and intelligent critic of some of liberalism's most sacred myths. That such a man can see this "anomaly" and not condemn it as a blot upon all that is presumably best in liberalism, even in that built upon "the diversity of human stories," is a sad commentary on what establishmentarian liberalism can do to the most keenly analytical mind.

Novak's concept of a political future in which liberal intellectuals and conservative ethnics will walk hand-in-hand is the heart of his message, and that is where conservatives must give him the attention he deserves. He knows the great strength of ethnic appeals and he also knows that liberalism as it now exists cannot hold the allegiance of the ethnics. He not only asks the ethnics to re-examine their drift toward the right, but asks his fellow liberals, even presumably the curiously Anglo-Saxon ones, to wise up and recognize that the future of the Democratic party depends to a great extent on recapturing the ethnics. His powers of diagnosis are excellent, but most ethnics, I believe, would look upon a prescription for more liberalism, even if coated with sugar, as bad medicine. Still, he has at least given the liberals a strategy and it is one which conservatives must pay attention to, not because it is correct, but because it might, if implemented, carry the day. There is, however, one fatal flaw in the strategy and conservative spokesmen must bring it to the attention of the ethnics:

If "ethnicity" is all that matters, then Novak and his political colleagues can well pull off a coup by plucking the ethnics from the rightward direction to which they have been slowly gravitating. A few references to goulash, a few visits to the local barroom à la Sarge Shriver, some "programs" geared to ethnics—and the liberal wing of the Democratic party can once more be able to count on the ethnic vote. But the liberals will not have changed in any substantive way. They will still be liberals, but only liberals who have enough sense to get out of the rain. Their point of view will continue to dominate a "new ethnic politics" in the Democratic party. They will, of course, be nice to ethnics but only because the ethnics are needed. The issue is not ethnicity, i.e., the background of the people, but their *beliefs*.

Stress ethnicity and you stress differences. Now this in itself is not bad. America needs more differences of this kind. But to stress only the differences is to leave the ethnic dependent, politically, on the politician who can "appeal" to certain ethnic characteristics. I share with Novak the belief that the melting-pot idea is historically inaccurate and not very good as an ideal either. It is, after all, a liberal idea and ideal. But ethnics can reject both the melting-pot and the ethnic ghetto. They can choose to remain ethnics and, at the same time, become conscious of the philosophical conservatism which they all share. I believe that is precisely what has happened with some members of ethnic groups in my own generation and the one directly after it.

Novak believes that the kind of conservatism I write of in this book is alien in style and dangerous in substance to ethnics. Yet, he himself writes: "The tradition of liberalism is a tradition I have had to acquire . . ."

But *why* does one have to "acquire" it and why should anyone from an ethnic background *want* to acquire it? Why buy the "reason, naked and undisguised, enlightenment" myths of contemporary liberalism at all? Is it because one cannot make it in the contemporary intellectual world without buying or seeming to buy these myths? If that is the case, why not say so? But don't, at the same time, ask those who have not bought the myths to follow you into the political party whose intellectual branch, and therefore most of its policies, is dominated by men and women who are the keepers of the myths.

While the liberals began to rediscover the virtues of the urban conservatives, the radicals were continuing their attack.

Garry Wills—the brilliant writer and columnist, who passed from conservatism of the *National Review* type directly into a fashionable radicalism, the kind that found the "kids" so wonderful in the late sixties, without going through the usual liberal phase—is the scourge of urban conservatives. In a column written in 1971, he denounced what he termed three "hypocrisies" on their part concerning the busing issue. He wrote:

> The busing dispute goes on with much hypocrisy. For one thing, we are given hymns to the concept of neighborhood. The

> neighborhood school is untouchable—this in a society where the father commutes to work, the mother wants a second car to drive around shopping centers, friends and family are scattered all over town and country. We deal in distances easily—to go purchase a bargain, to have things delivered, to reach places of work or recreation.

Wills sees a contradiction between being content to live in the suburbs and work in the city, i.e., to be willing to travel yourself, and being angry when your kids are involuntarily bused. Why this strikes Wills as hypocrisy is puzzling. It is perfectly consistent to be willing to endure the hardship of commuting for the good of your family while at the same time not be willing to have your children undergo the same hardship.

> A second hypocrisy hides behind the term "quality." We want a quality education, and any attention to social balance distracts from the pursuit of this goal. The funny thing is that this argument is now used by right-wing education critics like Max Rafferty and Russell Kirk, who have for years been telling us there is no quality in public schooling anyway. All of a sudden they do not want us distracted from a non-existent concern.

Once more, a curious reason to label the critics as hypocrites. One can very consistently state that public education has low quality and also state that busing will make it even lower. Why hypocrisy?

> A third hypocrisy centers on the phrase "forced integration." Integration would be all right if it happened as an accident, not on a plan, not imposed by courts. This argument assumes that there was a prior freedom of movement, and travel, and habitation, suddenly violated by the introduction of force.
>
> But the situation we now have, which calls for remedy, was created by force . . .
>
> The whole ghetto is an artificial and exploitative arrangement, at odds with the ideals we are supposed to be teaching in public schools. We owe it to ourselves to start breaking down the walls—and it is better that we do it with buses than with bombs.

If you are against "forced integration" you are a hypocrite because it was force that made segregation possible in the first place. Therefore, we should accept an unnatural arrangement, such as busing, because it was an unnatural arrangement that brought about segregation. Anyhow, it's either buses or bombs.

Wills is a New Bourbon, having learned or forgotten nothing. In 1974 he went to Boston, sniffed the South Boston area and declared its Irish inhabitants racist. They need civilizing; they live in a "jungle"—or so says Wills. Their opposition to forced busing brought on Wills' attack of intellectual bigotry.

It is this kind of radical logic, full of either/or threats that is helping the urban conservative to make up his mind about politics.

The liberal and radical intellectuals, then, are failing to regain the support of the urban conservatives because they continue to "utterly misinterpret the reality" of the neighborhoods and suburbs. But what about the Republican party, to which all of these political goodies should, by the nature of things, be flowing? Has it developed an attitude and a long-range plan to keep the urban conservative voters who ran from George McGovern in 1972? The disaster of 1974 seems to say no. But things aren't that simple. The Republican party can gain the support of urban conservative voters, but only if certain realities are understood. The first is that these voters are suspicious of Republicans.

When it was announced, in 1969, that I had been appointed to the White House staff as a writer, a Jersey City newspaper quoted my grandfather, Tim Gavin, eighty-year-old, retired street cleaner, staunch Democrat and magnificent human being, as saying: "I'm proud of my grandson. But I wish he wasn't working for a blankety-blank Republican."

When my mother showed me the clipping, she hastened to assure me that Grandpa had been misquoted. I knew better and was overjoyed that he had said it. It was exactly what I would have expected him to say and I would have been disappointed if he hadn't. The links to the Democratic party are strong in my family, on both sides, and it took an effort of the will for many of my relatives to adjust to the fact that I had gone over to what, from time immemorial, was considered the enemy. Grandpa Tim wasn't about to change the habits of a lifetime for one appointment, no matter how grand.

Yet street corner conservatism is, I believe, on the rise, and the transparent efforts of liberals of both parties won't stop it. The conservatives in the cities are being offered the same old liberal shell game: liberalism with a human face is to replace the ideology of the sixties. But liberalism's human face is ideological. There is not a single McGovern position during the 1972 Presidential campaign which did not have its origin in some basic liberal ideal or principle.[18] Now the liberals are saying that it wasn't liberalism that was rejected in 1972, it was McGovern.

The success of the liberals will be determined not by any policies or plans the group members may offer, but by whether they can fool old-line Democrats like Tim Gavin into believing that they have his interests at heart. In 1974 Hugh Carey demonstrated that this can be done effectively. As Evans & Novak pointed out during Carey's primary race:[19]

> Instead of combativeness, Carey strategists want nostalgic identification with the glorious past—not the dreary present—of the New York Democratic party . . .
>
> Carey, in short, is waging an essentially non-ideological campaign aimed at rebuilding the old Democratic coalition. . .

He certainly put the coalition together; whether he rebuilt it remains to be seen. A liberal will try anything, even common sense, to regain power, but is the "nostalgic identification with the glorious past" going to work? I don't think so.

Whether or not the Republican party is sharp enough to grasp this historic opportunity, I do not know. Watergate and its subsequent disclosures have, in effect, acted to stop the motion picture film of history. The 1974 Congressional elections went beyond that and (if I may conclude my cinematic metaphor) ran the film in reverse.

18. Hubert H. Humphrey, after saturation bombing of McGovern in the primary, was back during the campaign supporting the same policies he had previously declared anathema.

19. Evans & Novak, *Washington Post,* September 5, 1974.

There is now a curious kind of historical paralysis in what most political observers felt had been a steady drift of old-line Democrats into what was at least a thawing of relations with the ancient enemy as well as, in some cases, even mass defection of certain groups.

But Watergate and inflation stopped all that. The political wisdom of 1972 is of no use to anyone who attempts to predict where the urban conservatives can—or will—go. But this much is certain: they will never support a candidate for President who is an avowed liberal and they would, I believe, support the right kind of conservative. I have no polling data to prove this but I am convinced that the urban conservative heart has its secrets the pollsters can never know.

The question, then, is this: who is going to adapt more quickly to the reality of the 1970's—the Democratic party, which was for many years the urban conservative's natural home, or the Republican party, which on matters of principle has, for the most part, shown some signs of paying attention to the urban conservative's basic social outlook?

Watergate didn't make millions of Democrats who had defected to Nixon suddenly turn and see their old party through rose-colored glasses. The Democratic party is still the party of the liberals. Those liberals who are smart enough to know that McGovernism is the kiss of death might deserve some credit for common sense. Gary Hart became a Senator by running a campaign using rhetoric that seemed left over from early drafts of *The Conscience of a Conservative*. But such liberals are in no position to tell urban conservatives that this sudden blinding flash of sense has made liberalism the philosophy of the man on the street corner.

That the Republican party has been damaged by Watergate is a truism; but it is just as true, I think, that politics in general has been hurt. The question that political leaders in both parties might answer is whether they are prepared to adapt their parties to the challenge of conservatism. The Republicans simply can't count forever on the Democrats' ineptness at the Presidential candidate's level; and the Democrats cannot hope to get a Watergate every four years. What must be done must be done quickly and the party that shows, by action and words, that it is ready to accommodate itself to the needs and goals of conservatism will not only gain conservatives' votes, but their allegiance as well.

Can the Republicans do it? It would seem that the answer is no. Kevin Phillips, the first to write of urban conservatives as natural members of an emerging Republican majority, thought not. Writing in the *National Review* in December, 1972, of the battle between Democrats and Republicans to win the conservative vote, he stated:

> . . . This shift in political grudge warfare offers the GOP two chances: 1) the opportunity to mobilize conservative Democratic traditionalists against the Greening of America/New Politics crowd; and 2) the chance to hammer out a common philosophy of progress that will go beyond a shared negativism to a shared positive program for America. To date, the Nixon Administration has had some success in the first instance, and very little in the second.
>
> Here is where the deficiencies of many Republicans, and the managerial hierarchs in the Nixon Administration particularly, come into unfortunate prominence. For four years, a great philosophic and political opportunity has been staring the Nixon Administration in the face, and it has lacked the competence to grasp it . . .

Needless to say, Phillips was all too prophetic. Even if Watergate had never happened, the "managerial" approach of the Nixon administration would have turned off urban conservatives.

Just as the Democrats have made the mistake of seeing the urban conservative only as Economic Man, the Republicans have seen him too often only as Patriotic Man or Man With a Grudge. Now it is shrewd politics to exploit legitimate grievances. For a generation the Democratic party, for example, nominated Presidential candidates who ran against Herbert Hoover no matter whom the Republicans nominated. But there is a kind of short-sightedness about a politics that is *only* shrewd. There must be not only the exploitation of gripes but a positive, shared vision. The Republican party has thus far failed to provide that vision, as Phillips points out. I think that this failure can be traced in part to the short-term gain emphasis of the political strategists in the Nixon White House.

Intent upon election victories in 1970 and 1972, they placed the emphasis upon the shared commitment of the President and the urban conservatives to peace with honor abroad and safe streets at home. But no effort was made to consolidate this brief encounter of Republicans with urban conservatives and the only way it can be consolidated is to avoid seeing the urban conservative as an "issue" voter. The urban conservative is going to vote Republican only if the Republican party demonstrates it understands and appreciates the entire reality of the urban conservative experience. It simply will not do to push the "Patriot" button one week and the "Anti-Élitist" button the next. Indeed, there has to be an end to button-pushing—or at least an end to button-pushing when the finger pushing the button is always WASP, midwestern or Californian or wealthy. The urban conservative wants to be part of the decisions that are being made in his name.

Therefore, to speak of "urban conservatives" or "street corner conservatism" is not simply to invent yet another term to describe the invisible man. It is to state that the invisible man must be understood in his complete humanity, not as an economic problem or a social class or a social scientist's subject, but as a human being who has basic principles which affect his life much more than his economic, social or "ethnic" status.

Chapter 5

Crime, Race, Catholics and Reaction

CRIME

That evening, I boarded the suburban-bound bus at 17th and K Streets, a few blocks from my office. Rush-hour traffic in Washington is the same as rush-hour traffic in any big city: de-humanizing, mind-numbing, maddening. After we had crawled along at five miles an hour or so for a short distance, the bus stopped and a man dressed in neat denim working clothes got on. He was big, wide, obviously solid, and absolutely blind drunk.

He swayed for a moment, muttering something incoherent to the driver and then turned in drunken slow-motion to face those seated. I was sitting near the aisle opposite the rear door and I watched him as he very slowly and unsteadily made his way toward me, bumping into the few standing passengers, lurching back and forth as the bus heaved and jerked and crept its way toward the Virginia suburbs. As he approached my seat, he was talking in that unique combination of utter disorganization of ideas and complete clarity of diction that seem to be characteristic of certain drunks who have reached a rock-bottom of intoxication. He paused now and then to state to no one in particular:

"Hey . . . did you *read* . . . 'bout . . . the two *girls*? They got strangled! Yeah! I'm bad. Bad and *tough*. Tough!"

He finally reached my seat and sat down heavily alongside me.

Commuting by bus offers few pleasures but it does allow one to catch up on reading, so as soon as I get on a commuter bus I begin to read. On this evening I had been reading John Toland's *The Rising Sun*. The drunk suddenly placed his hand on my open book and slowly but firmly pushed it away from me.

"Did you read 'bout those two girls?"

"No," I said, "I didn't."

For a few seconds he stared at me (or perhaps through me) and then took his hand from the book. He stood up, turned, and began to stumble toward the front of the bus. He continued to talk about the "two girls" who had been "strangled." (Only a week before two girls *had* been murdered in Washington and the grisly deaths had made headlines.) He asked a few commuters if they knew how tough he was and if they had read about the two strangled girls. Then, suddenly, he was struck by a new idea. He turned and announced to all passengers in a sinister, menacing tone:

"The . . . Postman . . . Always . . . Ring . . . *Twice* . . . starring John *Garfield*! . . . The Postman Always Ring *Twice*!"

By this time the bus had reached M Street in Georgetown on the way to Key Bridge leading to Arlington. During rush-hour there are quite a few policemen directing traffic on M Street and, as we inched past them, it occurred to me that someone (the driver? I?) should ask a policeman to remove the drunk from the bus. After all, two girls murdered, The Postman Ringing Twice . . . maybe this guy is a killer. But foot-by-foot we passed cop after cop and nobody did anything.

Except the drunk. He suddenly shouted at the driver:

"Lemme off this bus! Lemme off!"

I could almost feel the sense of relief emanating from the other passengers and I most certainly became less tense myself. For approximately ten minutes this hulking, surly, drunken guy had been carrying on an effective, if probably unwitting, psychological terror campaign and now he was going to get off the bus.

But it didn't work out that way. The driver turned and said to him:

"Sir, I *told* you when you got on this bus that I'm not allowed to discharge passengers in Washington. You'll have to wait until we get to Virginia. I told you when you got on."

"Lemme off! Lemme off!"

"I'm sorry, sir, I can't let you off."

It was incredible. The driver, for legalistic reasons, was refusing to allow this maniac to get off. Passengers from every part of the bus began to shout at the driver:

"You goddamn fool. Let him *off*!"

"Let him go, let him off."

"Are you out of your mind? Let him off!"

But the driver, evidently a strict-constructionist of the old school, would not be dissuaded.

The drunk began once more to roam the aisle and asked if we had read about the two dead girls . . . this time adding a detail: they had been strangled with a "silk stocking"—pausing from time to time to very slowly state, "The Postman Always Ring Twice . . . starring John Garfield." I had a brief fantasy in which I politely asked him why he didn't give equal billing to Lana Turner and Hume Cronyn, each of whom had out-acted Garfield in that film—a fantasy I would have indulged only if motivated by a strong death wish. I was suffering from the mini-terror as much as anyone else and all I wanted was for the drunk to go away.

And he did . . . but only when we got across the Key Bridge and were in Virginia where commuter disembarkation is, thank God, legal. He bumped and rolled his way down the steps, and then turned to bid us fond *adieu*.

"Virginia . . . mah *home* state! The . . . Postman . . . Always . . . Ring . . . *Twice* . . ."

Starring John Garfield, no doubt, but he didn't bother to tell us that again. No sooner had he stepped off the bus than an angry—damn near hysterical—male voice rang out from the rear of the bus.

"Driver, what in the name of God is the *matter* with you. That madman might have killed us."

Shouts of agreement arose from all over the bus and a black woman now seated next to me nodded vigorously and shouted, "That's right! What's the *matter* with you?" to the driver.

The driver, all dignity and possessed of a self-assurance matched only by that of Oxford dons and maître d's, stopped the bus and, turning toward the rear, said:

"Sir, are you addressing me?"

"You're damned straight I'm addressing you," said the voice.

"Then perhaps you'd like to come up here and say that."

"You're damned right!"

He came past me, a nicely-dressed young man who could have easily passed for a professor of history or a middle-class bureaucrat, not the kind you expect to shout at bus drivers.

"Don't you realize that the man could have killed us? Let me off this bus and I'll go to the nearest police station. That guy might have been armed."

The driver wasn't having any, thank you.

"I'm forbidden to discharge passengers in Washington. I told him that when he got on the bus."

"But damn it, man," said the angry young man, "use your common *sense*. You could have called a policeman on M Street."

It seems as though that had occurred to almost everyone on the bus for I found myself shouting "that's right" with others.

"Would you have testified against the man in court?" asked the driver.

A heart-beat pause. And then:

"Certainly," the man answered . . . but in a tone just slightly less confident than before.

"Well I told him when he got on he'd have to stay on the bus," said the driver.

"Let me off here," the man said, "there's a police station nearby."

"I'll let you off at the proper stop," said the driver. And he did.

Not much of an incident as urban problems go these days. Nice material for an anecdote, perhaps, with the driver wearing bureaucratic blinders, the strange morbid mutterings of the drunk, a good story, part nightmare part farce, to tell—with emphasis on the delicious absurdity of it all—to dinner guests.

And yet there is something missing from the story as I have told it. That something is essential to understanding the incident and it is the feeling I had in the pit of my stomach or in the marrow of my bones or wherever it is that fear sits. I was, quite frankly, terrified of that drunk. I think that most discussions of urban violence and threats of violence are going to continue to be meaningless until that feeling is experienced by the experts. The incident was absurd, but it was also frightening. The fashionable word for the entire incident is "Kafkaesque" and in this case, unlike so many others where the word is misused, the word fits because at the heart of Kafka is not absurdity but unspeakable, bone-chilling terror.

The quite logical but totally irrelevant, indeed perverse, legalities of the driver, the stream-of-consciousness references to an old movie, the possibility that the drunk could have been trying to tell us all that he was the murderer—all of this was held together by a sense of shame and fright and psychological terror. We had boarded the bus as commuters and suddenly we were victims and there was nothing any of us could do about it.

"Would you have testified . . . ?" The driver's question stopped us all in our self-righteous anger at his legalistic stupidity. Would I have testified? Would I have risked going to court to look into the drunk's now-sober, all-remembering, unforgiving bloodshot eyes? And what would I have said if I had testified against the drunk? That he was a loyal John Garfield fan? No crime there, unless it is an aesthetic one. That he had threatened anyone? But he hadn't. That he was annoying? If that were a crime we'd all be in jail.

I don't know. The only way you can tell about those things is to get that *feeling*, a feeling of hopelessness and impotence and rage and fear that is at the heart of much of urban life today. It is a feeling that is too much to be borne for any length of time, and most city and suburban residents have lived with it much too long. Those who talk so piously and so definitively about "urban problems," and do so without having known that feeling first-hand, simply do not know what they are talking about. In the final analysis, it is that feeling which must be eliminated and until it is all the money and compassion and rhetoric in the world will not change our cities. I have spent more time on public transportation than I care to remember and I have endured more than my share of nasty midnight drunks on deserted subway cars and teen-age hoods out to prove their manhood by acting tough. But until quite recently, these disturbances, while annoying, were rarely terrifying.

Looking back, it wasn't the drunk or the letter-of-the-law driver or even the feeling of terror that made this incident memorable. It was the gnawing feeling that such an incident is no longer an isolated one, that things like this—and worse—are qualitatively different from similar incidents that happened over ten years ago and that the death of the cities might come about because the psychological price of living in the kind of atmosphere urban crime produces is becoming too high. All of the liberal rhetoric in the world won't make that psychological reality go away. Perhaps what is needed is a law making it mandatory for ritualistic liberals, especially those who pride themselves on being urban experts, to ride public transportation until they, in one way or another, find themselves confronted with that *feeling*. Once they experience it, they'll never be the same.

RACE

The incident on a city bus brought to mind the problem that many urban conservatives don't like to talk about: the accusations of racism leveled against them. The drunk on the bus happened to be black.

A poll taken for the *New York Times* by Daniel Yankelovich in November, 1973, showed that fully a third of black families in New York City identified themselves as "conservative." It would seem that there is a mutuality of interests between many black families and urban conservatives. Yet, "a tragedy of history" over which neither the urban conservatives nor black Americans had any control, has created a situation through the years in which the urban conservative, when he thinks of blacks at all, thinks of them in terms of violence. It is not fair. It is not morally right. But that's the way it is.

The drunk on the bus is, unfortunately, a symbol of "*black* violence" rather than violence as such. There is no use wasting time making the same old condescending remarks about the overwhelming majority of black Americans being law-abiding. Indeed, I think it is insulting to do so. The fact is that there is great tension between the two communities. It shouldn't be that way and I don't think it will remain that way. But that's the way it is and there is no use pretending. The only rational thing to do is to begin asking the right questions and the major one is the one that the Kerner Commission Report has made an official part of the American story: Are white Americans racist? More specifically: Are urban conservatives racist?

Is there any truth to the charges of racism among urban conservatives? In a sense, there is. Or, rather, such charges are partly true because "racism," unless it means anything one wants it to mean (like "genocide"), has a specific meaning: "A belief that human races have distinctive makeups that determine their respective cultures, usually involving the idea that one's own race is superior and has the right to rule others." Using this definition, anyone who lived in an urban neighborhood could tell you that "racism" simply did not exist there, if for no other reason than the average working man had too much on his mind, what with work and the kids and the wife and the bowling and the television and a few beers now and then. He simply didn't have time to create or understand or even think about a conscious theory of white racial superiority. Racism? Not in the neighborhoods.

But this doesn't let the urban conservative off the hook. There was, and is, animosity toward blacks. Anyone who denies that is either a liar or a propagandist for some ethnic group. There is animosity and it ranges in strength from mild, off-and-on abusive comments about alleged Negro failings to a virulent, incredibly bitter hatred of all blacks. This must be admitted by urban conservatives and any attempt to dismiss its existence is foolish. But the fault is *human*, not ideological, i.e., the kind of animosity I am talking about has its roots in the human condition, not in some well-thought-out philosophy of race.

To those who do not see the distinction, or who see it and are not convinced it matters, I can only say that I think there is a difference in kind, not in degree, between racism and race animosity. We deplore both, but we must be able to make the intellectual distinction between the two, because the second —the unthoughtful, off-and-on kind of race animosity, even in its most virulent form—*is*, despite its obvious bad effects, within the range of what most people would call normal human behavior.

To be normal, as the Church has so often reminded us, is not always to be good, but to be normal is at the very least not to be abnormal, diseased, twisted out of human shape. "The human condition" is, of course, an easy way of explaining—or explaining away—almost anything. Yet intellectuals, who have a sacred duty to make intellectual distinctions, do not make this one and I think that much of the animosity at the highest (that is, more virulent) end of the scale which characterized the late sixties came about, not because of some racist spot on a man's urban white soul, but because he was sick of hearing what he considered normal, if not admirable, behavior denounced as a form of racist ideology.

In the urban neighborhoods one hears "nigger" and one hears "whitey" or "the man." White workers bitch about blacks and blacks bitch about whites. Poles don't like the Irish and the Irish are convinced that heaven looks like a Saint Patrick's Day Parade. Ethnics of one group are certain that ethnics of another group are stupid or lazy or something else by nature—and yet, it all seems to work. They live together, they work together, they enjoy each other's company when that company has some kind of unpressured, happy reason for being.

At the same time they go home and complain about that stupid Polack or that Jew bastard. This is not what the moral theology textbooks tell us should happen. But it does happen. How to overcome this phenomenon I do not know, but to label it "racism" is irresponsible. There is animosity of this kind, although expressed in nicer language, for Catholics among liberal intellectuals, just as there is for blacks among urban conservatives, but no one ever calls the liberal intellectuals bigoted.

To all of this there are, and will always be, great, admirable exceptions. There are liberal intellectuals who have learned that a man can embrace Catholicism while at the same time being as intellectually respectable as themselves. There are working men and women who have learned that a black man may talk "funny" and eat "funny" food and do a lot of "funny" things but is still a good guy. There are Catholics who are closed-minded and there are blacks who are violent—closed-mindedness and violence being what the liberals and urban conservatives fear most about the Catholics and blacks respectively—and so long as there are, there will be those, both liberal intellectuals and urban conservatives, who will make sterotypes of all Catholics and blacks. But this is the phenomenon we are dealing with . . . *not* institutional or philosophical racism.

What can be done about it? I don't know. I think that the kind of discussion group ecumenism that liberals seem to engage in with no discernible misgivings is not the kind of thing that urban conservatives can do without feeling that the whole thing is phony. The fact of the matter is that black Americans are not particularly desirous of moving next door to me, but that, understandably enough, they don't want me to have the power to keep them from doing so. I think urban conservatives understand that kind of logic because it doesn't deal with theoretical abstractions but with common sense.

I do not know if urban conservatives and black Americans can live in peace and harmony. I do know that there is no liberal solution to the problem of race that has made it easier for the conservatives or the blacks. I think that most white people, when left to their own devices, tend to think of blacks as a group (and vice versa). Perhaps in a few years it will be seen that urban conservatives who are family-oriented have much more in common with black families of their own economic class than either of them do with the liberal ideologues who tell them what is supposedly best for them. But then, too many have offered a solution to the problems of race. I think the best thing conservatives can do is to admit it exists but that it is different in kind from the "racism" problem so doted-on by liberal sociologists and propagandists.

CATHOLICS

1964 was a bad year. I was living in a suburb of Philadelphia at the time and rooting for the Phillies. Baseball fans will remember that year as one in which the Phillies, going into the last week of the season with a comfortable first-place lead, went into a slump unmatched in modern times for slow-motion agony. The Phillies found at least 16 new ways to lose ball games, quite a feat for a club whose record since the beginning of organized baseball is atrocious. They blew it.

And, of course, there was the Barry Goldwater campaign. I can remember standing on a windy and, alas, almost deserted street corner in Philadelphia, listening to, yes, vice-presidential candidate Bill Miller (you can look it up) and Mrs. Bill Miller addressing a group (the Goldwater team didn't draw crowds in Philadelphia, just groups) of winos, disgruntled teenagers looking for some action, and me. This was what was known as a "rally." Why Miller came to Philadelphia, where the Goldwater candidacy was looked upon with, let us say, skepticism, and what Miller said that night, I can't recall. All I can recall is a strange looking character standing next to me, muttering to himself in some foreign language.

That was the way the Goldwater campaign went in Philadelphia. Barry, God bless him, had given a hint as to the rhetorical direction of the campaign when, earlier along the trail, he addressed a group of the faithful on the steps of a suburban restaurant, the Casa Conti in Abington, the town where I was living at the time. That was the place Barry chose to complain, aloud, that minorities had too much influence in this country. The Republican candidates for office standing on the platform with him turned green, made gargling sounds . . . and, for the most part, were never heard from again. It was that kind of year.

My most vivid memory of 1964, however, concerns a long, often ferocious discussion I had with a fellow teacher. He couldn't understand why I was supporting Goldwater. Finally, in exasperation, he shouted, "How can you, a *Catholic,* vote for that man?"

I eventually did vote for Barry and would again. No angel of death visited me—as far as I know—and my religious orthodoxy remains unsullied. Yet that question spoke volumes. My colleague represented the liberal approach to religious and political affairs, and conservatives must confess that, in recent years, this approach has won the day. The unspoken premise behind his question was: "How can you be an intelligent Catholic in our age and not be a liberal?"

The Roman Catholic church has survived persecution, friends in high places, German theologians, Irish-American monsignors, Italian Popes, French kings, dictators of all sorts, heresies, schisms, *Commonweal* magazine and even bingo. It will no doubt survive its current troubles. Yet, for the kind of conservatives about whom this book is written, these have been trying times. Man and boy, I have attended Sunday Mass all my life and I never heard anyone, anywhere, ever mention that what we all needed was a change in the liturgy.

I'm certain that such a change was lusted after by some theologians, liberal Catholic intellectuals and the kind of back-to-the-land crowd Eugene McCarthy belonged to in the fifties. But real people? We never said a word. We were satisfied. Yet, one day we all woke up to discover that there was ostensibly a desperate longing throughout the Church universal for Mass to be said in the vernacular. I will confess there have been times when I have dozed during a sermon but surely the great need for Mass in English could not have been discussed publicly only when I was in dreamland.

But this is a twice-told tale. Who has not heard by now the complaints of those who view with horror a translation of scripture that speaks of the woman who lost a "dime" and spent the day searching for it (I actually once heard this version of the good news preached), and of those blue meanies who feel the addition of the guitar Mass did not add to the spiritual heritage of the West? I have reached the point where I actually like some of the guitar music, and the wild scriptural translations into English have, in recent years, been toned down. I am not averse to performing my Sunday religious duty on Saturday evenings, and I am extending the peace of the Lord to my pew-mates with less anger and embarrassment these days. No, this street corner conservative, while still angry at some of the changes that have been made, has adjusted, I believe, to the new ways. We have Christ's promise after all, and the gates of Hell (and, by extension, liberal theologians) shall not prevail against us.

True conservatism, in the Church as well as in politics, resembles the act of a tightrope walker. In order to remain where you want to be you have to make small movements of adjustment from time to time. Thus, despite some of the more widely-publicized horrors that were visited upon the faithful by over-zealous, liberal, religious bureaucrats in recent years, no urban or street corner conservative I know feels that the post-Vatican Two world has been a total disaster area.

There are those who call themselves conservatives who choose to spend their time shouting ferocious slogans in Spanish (Spain, you see, is the Eden of the Orthodox-Chic set), bad-mouthing the United States as a decadent nation unworthy of Christian support, and generally giving the impression that the Second Coming will occur only when everyone learns to speak Latin. These are spiritual descendants of the same old crowd that John Henry Newman had to defend himself against during the nineteenth century, the more-Catholic-than-the-Pope spiritual shock troops of reaction.

Street corner conservatives, faced with the blunders, the arrogance and the lack of Christian charity which signify contemporary liberal and radical Catholicism, can sympathize with the hate-America reactionaries, but I am convinced that conservatives can best get the Church back on course by continuing to walk the tightrope.

If all this seems terribly, well, parochial to the reader of another faith, I think it might be necessary to add that I believe the fate of the Catholic Church in the United States is probably the most important problem confronting the conservatives I write of. The common sense and common decency of urban conservatives are needed in the Church where both sense and decency have been missing in controversies during recent years. The Catholic Church in the United States is, with the exception of some bishops and, I believe, a majority of parish priests, dominated by liberal bureaucrats. Quite a bit of the Catholic school system is; many diocesan offices of education most certainly are.

Fifteen years ago, if anyone had said that in a few years the Church would be considered a "problem" area for urban conservatives, the prediction would have been greeted with laughter. No one is laughing now. As usual, the conservatives were not asked if they wanted "change." They woke up one day and were told that they wanted it. In-the-pew conservatives were not consulted about the liberal direction of the Catholic schools and Catholic education in general. They suddenly discovered that their Church had embraced with the fervor of the convert educational theories which, even as they were being espoused by the Catholic schools, were being dropped by the liberals as disasters. Innovation, how many educational sins have been committed in your name!

So the conservatives continue to walk the tightrope. There are those who want conservatives to lean all the way to the left side, and others calling for a total shift to the right. But the conservatives, in Church affairs as well as politics, know that in order to keep one's balance, there must be an avoidance of sudden movement but, at the same time, a continuing series of little adjustments are necessary to keep one from falling. It is not the easiest way of life, but it is the only one open to conservatives in spiritual or political matters.

REACTION

Through previous sections of this book I have argued that urban conservatives have been misunderstood or ignored by politicians and the media. I think the same can be said of the conservative intellectual movement as a whole. Despite such shows as Buckley's *Firing Line* and a sprinkling of conservative intellectuals throughout the universities, conservatism as an intellectual force has received short shrift from the establishment. The situation is not now so bad as it once was—after all, Guy Davenport reviews for the *New York Times Book Review* which is, in turn, edited by John Leonard who, although no conservative, did begin with the *National Review* and at least understands the arguments—but it still is a scandal.

Whatever the reason—a subtle, never-stated but universal quota system working against intellectual conservatives or (and this is my guess) simply the fact that liberals tend to hire people they know or like or both and that these people tend to be liberals also in the nature of things—whatever the reason, conservative intellectuals are not at all represented in anything like their full strength in the prestigious universities, publications and in the media. It is a liberal's world, the world of the mind in the United States.

And yet, anyone who has observed the conservative movement for even a short time gets the feeling that there is more to the problem than merely the depravity of liberals. Could it not be that part of the problem is not with the liberals, or not wholly so at any rate, but with conservatives themselves? Could it possibly be that there is something about the conservative intellectual movement in the United States that tends to inhibit the kind of atmosphere in which a fullblooded, lusty intellectual conservative could grow and prosper?

These questions are not, as you have already guessed, merely rhetorical. The more I read the writings of, and talk to, conservative intellectuals the more I am convinced that there is a *malaise* in the conservative intellectual community which cannot be blamed on liberal quotas or the very real prejudices against conservatives as intellectuals.

To paraphrase Robert Frost, there is something in the conservative intellectual movement that loves a wall, a wall that keeps the uncleansed, the unshriven and the unwanted from staining the pure, unsullied dogmas handed down to conservative intellectual chieftains from the days of old. In short, no traffic is permitted with intellectuals who are not prepared to take the vows of intellectual poverty, chastity and obedience that conservative ideological supporters demand,. It is a far, far better thing to read aloud to yourself from the works of Von Mises than, say, to invite Norman Podhoretz to a conservative function or to publicly praise Irving Kristol or any of a dozen or so liberal intellectuals who are not of the one true faith but whose work in recent years has in one way or another reflected values that conservatives once thought were exclusively theirs. I hasten to add that this is not my criticism alone, but that of many young conservative intellectuals I have gotten to know during the past ten or so years.

Now I understand that what I have said here about conservatives can just as easily and much more truthfully be said about liberals and left-radicals. Of *course* they run a closed intellectual shop. Of *course* they deal in dogmatics instead of using the intellectual process to achieve rational ends of rational men. Of *course* liberals and the radical left have made a mockery of true intellectuals while at the same time claiming to speak for all those who desire to follow the life of the mind.

These are all the more reasons why there should be an investigation into the desirability of the conservative movement opening its ranks to the moderate center-left. By now we expect dogmatism, fanaticism and the lesser forms of intellectual conformity from the left. But we should be shocked when it appears on the right, and I fear we are not. A young libertarian intellectual once told me he was not going to a local meeting of a well-known conservative intellectual group because he had looked at a list of the panelists and had concluded he knew what they were going to say because they were the same people he had been talking to for the past half-dozen years. What they said when he first met them was pretty much what they were saying now, so what was the use of attending?

And what are the intellectual cubby-holes into which the conservative movement has divided itself? I think they can best be understood as types:

1. *The Conservative as Eighteenth Century Freak.* He can't stand the twentieth century. He doesn't think much of the nineteenth century either. But the eighteenth had certain charms (those country-houses were delightful), and people knew their places. A few thousand pounds a year, his wool spun for him by an old family retainer and he would spend the rest of his days reading Edmund Burke in a Latin translation (this type loves his Latin). He hates cities, all mechanical objects and any group of over ten people. A good education means Latin and Greek, a smattering of the Bible, perhaps a dash or two of the Book of Common Prayer and *discipline.* He likes people to tip their hats and mind their manners. He loves little things and hates big things. When you ask him to name his favorite modern novel, he'll say *Sense and Sensibility.* And every now and then he wonders aloud why so many young Americans think conservatives are irrelevant.

2. *The Conservative as Economic Tough-Guy.* No nonsense, this fellow. Either you make it or you don't. You cut the mustard or fall by the wayside. Name an economic cliché and this guy has used it six times this week. Conservatism to him means property and property means money and them that has gets and them that don't, don't and, sure as hell, don't deserve any of *his* hard-earned money. He sneers at those who don't understand the value of a dollar, and at those who do understand the value of a poem. He knows what the world is all about and if you haven't met a payroll what the hell do you know about it, sonny? Every now and then he sighs and wishes that the coming generation would have enough sense to convert to his way of life.

3. *The Conservative as Individualist.* A bit of a crank to most people, he sees himself as the last outpost of individualism in a world of creeping collectivism. He is so individualistic he doesn't want you to be what you want to be; he wants you to

be what he wants to be, i.e., a man apart. Anyone who applauds a movement or program that has been created by, and that will appeal to or benefit, more than one person, he scorns as a member of the pack, living by the herd instinct. He hates all government, especially big government. In fact, he hates *anything* big. In this regard he resembles his Eighteenth Century Freak conservative brother, but the individualist hates bigness just because it is big, not simply because it is modern. He hates unions, taxes, movies, jazz, rock, television, the telephone, cars and crowds. He writes letters to the newspapers in which he demands to know why all young people don't recognize the values of individualism in the same way he does.

4. *The Conservative as Keeper of the Flame.* You are at a cocktail party and you mention that once, in a moment of weakness, you had a moment of admiration for Bobby Kennedy's courage. The Flame-Keeper pins you to the wall and demands to know if you fully understand what you are saying. Bobby Kennedy? My God, man. This guy has memorized every conservative position on every political and social subject since the death of Edmund Burke and woe to him who deviates from The Conservative Line. He hasn't changed an opinion in thirty years and every now and then he complains that leftist kids today don't have open minds.

5. Then there is *Young Conservative Playing Bill Buckley*—complete with winking, blinking eyes, almost-British accent and darting tongue. The trouble with this role is that there is, alas, only one Bill Buckley and imitations of his style very often make the would-be imitator sound and look like early Ronald Colman with a twitch.

I have been told that my list is not complete unless it includes another type: *Conservative as Romantic-Irish-Catholic-Urban Primitive*. Since I don't know anyone who fits that type-casting I must, alack, leave it out of my list.

If the idea of conservatism is to keep the riff-raff out, to keep it a small club of those who sip sherry and speak in cultured tones about the well-deserved doom of Western civilization, then the need to fit all conservatives into one or another of these types (or reasonable facsimiles thereof) is understandable. But—if conservatism is to be a movement which seeks not to comment eloquently upon the decline of the West, but rather to stop that decline; if it seeks not to keep conservatism a club for Ivy League types and eccentrics and hard-hitting free-entrepreneurs, but rather to make it a home for intelligent young men and women who are sick of liberalism, disgusted with left radicalism but not quite certain which way to turn—then there must be an effort to broaden not the base but the very *concept* of conservatism.

The course of the decade of the seventies in general, and the events of the election year of 1976 in particular, are going to be determined by many young men and women who have not yet chosen an intellectual path, and who just might turn to conservatism if it doesn't look cramped, gloomy and forbidding. This is not a call for electric guitars as background to Burke and mini-skirts as foreground for free-enterprise, but a plea for a new look at what it means to be a conservative in general and a conservative intellectual in particular.

Chapter 6

What Is It That You People Want, Anyway?

A couple of years ago a Roman Catholic priest named Geno Baroni appeared on a local television interview program in Washington. Monsignor Baroni in those days was devoting much of his time to crusading for better treatment for ethnic groups and, on the program, he had given the three interviewers a detailed explanation of the grievances of white urban ethnics.

Toward the end of the show, one of the interviewers, an attractive, young, articulate, black woman leaned across to Monsignor Baroni, her face showing extreme puzzlement.

"I've listened very carefully to you," she said, or words to this effect, "but I'm still not certain as to what you people want."

She missed the unintentional irony. Here was a black woman, presumably doubly discriminated-against, asking a white ethnic what he wanted. Only a few years ago, intelligent, articulate, white people were asking the same question of people of her race and sex and background.

The question still remains: What is it that urban conservatives want? I would think that one of the things they want is to be understood in their widest dimension, i.e., the philosophical, and to get out of the "ethnic" trap into which many well-meaning persons, including themselves, have placed them. Urban conservatives have wider and deeper interests than "ethnics" and, at the same time, have means at their disposal to see to it that their wants can be translated into action. Politics may have an ethnic element but it is a philosophy which determines the limits of that element. It is in the best interests of ethnic and blue-collar spokesmen to examine their preconceptions concerning the best ways to get the most and the best for their people. Urban conservatism transcends mere ethnicity and blue-collarism.

I know that many urban conservatives feel about politics the same way Marianne Moore felt about poetry: "I too dislike it; there are things that are important beyond all this fiddle." Politics in its purest form is interesting to relatively few human beings. Most of us have concerns that are at once closer and more important to us than mere politics. The fate of our family, the fate of our soul take up a great deal of our time. Work. Leisure. These are things that can take up the better part of a lifetime, if attended to with care and devotion.

Yet politics remains—outside the normal life of most urban conservatives, but still there—waiting to disturb or re-direct or otherwise change the normal channels of our lives. If we ignore politics for too long, those who don't ignore it suddenly become involved in our lives in ways we never thought possible. Yet, if we concentrate all our energies on politics, we one day discover that the very reason we are concentrating on politics—the good of our families and our neighborhoods—is being threatened or neglected due to our political pre-occupations.

It is a difficult decision. Liberals seem to have no trouble in adjusting to the rigors of political life. Many wealthy people, liberal and conservative, thrive on the dull, dreary, dehumanizing rituals that politics demands. But urban conservatives really don't like politics except, of course, in the case of the Irish and even they seem to be losing their interest in, if not their grip on, political matters.

In recent years, however, there have been unmistakable signs that it is in the long-range interest of urban conservatives to play a greater part in politics on the local, state and national levels. The busing controversy, abortion-on-demand, crime in the streets, the disruption of schools because of violence, the counter-culture barrage of indecency and hedonism—these have hit the urban conservative where he lives . . . in his home, his neighborhood, his school, his church.

There is a special irony to the urban conservatives' new-found interest in politics. Just at the time when they are re-discovering the need to take an interest, to "know the issues," some liberals are beginning to tell us that elections, after all, don't make any difference. In the words of one intellectual in 1972:

> As we have just seen, one danger in a Presidential election is that numerous Americans will take it seriously. Many suffer a tendency to think there is some *connection* between the election and future events. This sets the stage for sure frustration. Yet one has seen citizens flaunting lapel buttons and determined jaws as though convinced they are striving hand-in-hand with destiny. So the danger is real.[20]

In short, anyone who is foolish enough to think that his vote in a national election really determines anything in the *real* world is . . . well, he isn't an intellectual, that's for certain. The reason for some liberals' new-found disenchantment with the old political institutions and virtues was best described by Father Andrew Greeley in an article written after the McGovern fiasco:

> It is not merely that most liberals are too intellectually arrogant to admit that they might have made mistakes and that they might have totally misunderstood what was going on in the country.

20. "The Shape of Things as They Really Are" by Frank Trippett, *Intellectual Digest*, December, 1972.

More important, perhaps, is the liberal's need to feel morally superior. Ignorant and uninformed people have beaten him in an election. He is angry, bitter, frustrated. Why have they not recognized his superior intelligence? Why have they not granted him the power of government to which his obvious excellence entitles him?

The poor, stupid fools have in effect denied his intellectual brilliance. What else does he have left besides his moral superiority? At least they cannot take that away from him . . .

The 1974 off-year elections showed that the liberal post-McGovern *tristesse* has worn off. The liberals are back bringing the Good News of liberal programs and policies to those who have drifted away from the one true church of the genteel left. What I have written in this book about the suspicious character of much of the new-found liberal interest in urban conservatives was reflected in an article by Irving Kristol in the *Wall Street Journal*:

All of a sudden, we are being inundated by learned accounts of the "blue-collar blues." What happened? Why the intense interest in this subject at this time? Are the workers rioting in the streets? Burning down the factories? No, nothing so spectacular has occurred. What did happen is really quite prosaic: A great many workers, last year, decided to vote for George Wallace and subsequently for Richard Nixon, and for some liberal social scientists and politicians this "perverse" behavior requires deep sociological explanation . . .

While the liberal search for the cause of this "perverse" behavior goes on, the urban conservatives will have time to reexamine their own beliefs and start translating their social and moral philosophy into political action. First, however, it will be necessary to discover just what it is they want.

I can only guess what this might be, but I offer the following as a beginning of an answer:

Urban conservatives want something liberals and liberalism are not willing or able to give them. They want to be left alone.

The urban conservative may seem at first, like Garbo, to be bizarre. But consider: of all identifiable groups in the United States it is the urban conservatives who have not banded together for lobbying purposes. Ethnic groups proliferate among them and Catholic men's and women's organizations abound, but these are primarily social groups, mostly looking inward to their own memberships and touching upon the outside world only when the outside world touches them. Blacks have pressure groups—and well they should. Jews have pressure groups—and have been amazingly successful. Liberals know how to manipulate these groups because the groups act in a way that liberals understand and, to a great degree, are able to control. The tendency toward acting as a united group toward some definite social or political goal is an inclination liberals have a "feel" for. Social and political action directed toward social and political improvement (usually defined in terms of economic gains or civil liberties) has been the beating heart of contemporary liberalism.

But the urban conservatives don't want anything, except to be left alone, to live their own lives. They don't want to change the world, except that small part of it which is familiar to them—their homes, their neighborhoods—and even this kind of change must be slow. They don't want to make drastic changes in society because, unfashionable as it might seem, they like the structure of society as it is. They are constantly scolded for this tendency to be content with the existing social structure in the United States, but they know what they know and they want what they want, and what they want is a little bit more of what they already have for themselves and a chance of material betterment for their children.

During the nineteen-sixties, they were chastised from the pulpit and lectern over their lack of concern for the downtrodden. What the preachers and the professors did not know—and could not know, since they never talked with urban conservatives, only talked at them—was that the worst possible way to have urban conservatives join the various wars against poverty, distress, ignorance, illiteracy or whatever, was to demand that they join as members—enlisted men, of course—of the righteous, do-gooder army of liberalism. When asked to contribute to a church collection on Sunday ("The second collection will be for those who are hungry and poor"), the urban conservatives poured forth millions because the money was going through a channel they knew and trusted, i.e., the Church. But demands that they "join in the struggle against injustice"—the kind of vague, pietistic, abstract demand liberals thrive on—resulted in urban conservatives doing what they always have done when asked to act in a way that liberals insist is correct . . . they turned their backs.

Urban conservatives want to be left alone not because they are "xenophobic" but because what they have is world enough for them. To be able to work, to watch their children grow, to know that they can provide for their families, to "live and let live"—this may not be a profound social philosophy, but it is a way of life. Only when there are threats to that way of life do urban conservatives act. Even then they rarely act as a group. The march of the hard-hats in 1970, in favor of President Nixon during the Cambodian crisis, was startling not because there were so many of them or because they did extraordinary things during their march, but because they marched at all. Students march in protest. Peace advocates march in protest. Blacks march in protest. Everybody seems to march in protest except the urban conservatives, who march only when they want to show how happy they are, e.g., Saint Patrick's Day parades. When urban conservatives, wearing hard-hats, marched in support of the President and in protests against student violence and disruption, it was as if the sun had come up in the north. It was against nature, the nature of the urban conservative.

Sir Herbert Butterfield, Regius Professor Emeritus at the University of Cambridge, has written in the *New York Times:* "The key to everything—even perhaps to the emergence of the extraordinary criminal—lies in the mediocre desires, the intellectual confusions and the willful moods of the average man, the man in the street."

No better evidence can be found of the gap that exists between intellectuals, even such a distinguished and honored one as Sir Herbert, and the "man in the street" than this extraordinary sentence. It is precisely the desires, the confusions and the moods of intellectuals themselves which have, by and large, played a destructive role in changing the world in the modern era. The man in the street has wanted nothing but the chance to have what he has, to get a bit more, and to make certain his children have the chance to get even more. This may not be the path to heaven or to earthly paradise but it is enough for urban conservatives. Charity, compassion, a thirst for justice? They abound among urban conservatives but since they are rarely demonstrated in the ways judged by liberals to be correct, i.e., through public, usually governmental channels, directed and controlled by liberals, the urban conservatives are held to be lacking in these qualities.

All right, so the urban conservatives want to be left alone in peace and justice and safety so they can build their own lives. How does this make them different from everybody else?

Well, in one sense it doesn't. Everyone, or almost everyone, wants these things. But the leading liberal politicians and intellectuals during the past ten or fifteen years have not wanted these simple things. They have wanted social change —without thinking of asking the permission of the urban conservatives who would be hit by the change—in education and housing and just about everything else. I do not deny that this desire for change often came from worthy motives; nor do I deny there are many things in American society that need changing. But the liberals have demonstrated beyond any reasonable doubt that their way of bringing about change simply doesn't work or, at best, works to produce so many bad side effects that our society cannot afford them any longer.

There is a deep and permanent gulf between urban conservatives and liberal intellectuals and politicians. From time to time, on certain economic matters that gulf has been bridged. But the bridge is temporary. There are more reasons for urban conservatives to continue their rightward movement than there are for them to reverse course and try to get across that philosophical gulf. The gulf was made by the liberals although they won't admit it. *Newsweek* reported in January, 1973, a new three "r's" in schools across the country: "rape, robbery and riot." It is disingenuous for the liberals to deny that their attitudes toward education and toward urban conservatives had nothing whatsoever to do with this breakdown in the educational system.[21]

Since the liberals control the media and the publishing houses and the universities, they will no doubt re-write history to show that they had nothing to do with the breakdown. But the urban conservatives know better. They know it where it counts . . . in their bones, deep in the marrow where all the left-liberal propaganda in the world isn't going to penetrate. The liberal êlite have abused and neglected and philosophically attacked the urban conservatives too long for the urban conservatives to forget about it. The gulf is there. It is unbridgeable on most matters and on the old economic matters it is fast becoming unbridgeable.

Where does this leave the urban conservatives? Well, it leaves them with a better idea of who they are. Not a complete idea, but a better one than they had when their heart said one thing and their tradition of politics told them another. But knowing what you don't want (liberalism) is not the same as knowing what you want.

If I had a chance to talk to urban conservatives and street corner conservatives about conservatism, I would say this:

Our allegiance must not be to the forms of the past but to its virtues. If some of the forms of the past—institutions, traditions, political parties—still retain their virtues we should support them. If they do not, we should seek new ways to keep alive the virtues that no longer inspire the dying institutions. Demagogic pleas for a return to the past should be rejected

21. Nathan Glazer, writing of the campus disturbances of the sixties, said: "The universities now suffer from the consequences of an untempered and irrational attack on American society, government, and universities, one to which we as academics have contributed, and on which we have failed to give much light. The students who sat-in, threw out the deans, and fought with the police, have, after all, been taught by American academics, among others—by C. Wright Mills, Herbert Marcuse, Noam Chomsky, and many, many others. All these explained how the world operated, and we failed to answer effectively. Or we had forgotten the answers. We have to start remembering and start answering."

What he wrote about the universities can now be said also of the schools. Nathan Glazer, *Remembering the Answers*, Basic Books, 1970 (p. 306).

out of hand unless we know exactly what it is we are going back to.

The intellectuals tell us that we are turning our back on our heritage if we turn our back on liberal candidates. To them we say: It is you who turned your back on us. Your liberal candidates forgot us when there were other, more pleasing prospects in view. Not only that, the liberals forgot what it is to be liberal. They became an élite as arrogant and as pompous and as dangerous to our interests as the old Big Business we fought against in the thirties.

The Republican party wants us to come aboard but it is not quite certain what to make of us. There is only one thing we demand: that we are not made fools of. Don't press the Patriotic button or the Anti-liberal button again and again and expect us to be thankful for the thoughtfulness in asking for our allegiance. We are here to stay and we want to be seen as a kind of American, not simply as political automatons who, since they once voted automatically one way, can now be expected to vote automatically the other.

We were loyal to our unions and in most cases still are. But have our unions been loyal to us? Do they still fulfill any function for us as conservatives? As Americans? Are there other ways of helping our families and our friends that do not depend on the total domination of a given craft or industry by an organization that won't let people work unless they belong? Remember: we were once the victims of exploitation by some business bosses. Should we not examine the situation as it really is today, not as high-salaried myth-makers in the labor hierarchy tell us it is?

We are not beholden to business—big, small or medium. We owe business nothing but a fair price for its services. Just as we shouldn't depend on old economic reflexes in new economic situations as far as the unions are concerned, so with business. Sure, big business needs an eye kept on it always and everywhere. But so long as there are those who tell us that business is our natural enemy, our sons and daughters are going to think that business isn't for them. Let's look at business for what it is: a way of making money. Maybe we should start making some of that money ourselves instead of using our energies trying to help liberal intellectuals stop others from making money. If this is crass materialism, let the liberal intellectuals sell their summer cottages; let the college professors cut off their consultant fees: let John Kenneth Galbraith stop flying to Switzerland. Then, and only then, will we stop looking for material comfort in a legitimate way.

We have sent an awful lot of our sons to fight and die for this country. Let's not kid ourselves. Most of us didn't like the military life. It's not our way, for the most part. But we also know that it is a tough world and that the military is all that is standing between us and a lot of people who would do this country as much harm as they could. We are not, God knows, militarists. But why should we listen to the demagogic yodels of our alleged liberal friends who tell us that we don't need so much defense? We aren't getting anything out of defense—except a chance to be what we want to be, which is a hell of a lot more than a lot of our friends and relatives in certain nations of Europe have had for a generation.

That doesn't mean we let the generals get anything they want. We don't become generals too often. We drive generals around quite a lot, but the star rarely appears on our shoulders. So let's elect hard-headed guys who know that the world is tough but who can be tough with the military as well as with the welfare boys.

The same kind of intellectual who is telling us now that we were immoral to get into Vietnam was the guy who, in the nineteen-thirties and forties, was licking Stalin's boots while we were premature anti-Communists. He was wrong then; he is wrong now. The Vietnam war immoral? Maybe—but only if the war against fascism was immoral because there hasn't been a single incident condemned in Vietnam that didn't occur, in spades, in Germany.

We have a lot to offer but we also have a lot to learn. Our future depends not only on our understanding our own best interests but in acknowledging that our philosophical opponents, the liberals and left-radicals, are masters of the intellectual con game. We have to know the questions and the answers to dozens and scores of problems we were content to ignore.

Race? Look, we are not exactly paragons of inter-racial harmony. But, we aren't hypocrites like the liberals either, and we are sick of seeing the liberals use our money to make us feel guilty for mis-deeds against black Americans. But we should want justice if only because injustice can switch direction very easily, as the liberals learned to their sorrow in the sixties. If you want justice, act justly. It is as simple as that. This means you avoid the liberal fools whose solutions to racial injustices are worse than the problems and also avoid the guys who are trying to be cute with the racial issue.

Crime? We were the first to come up against the full, undisguised, and by now universally recognized, onslaught of the new barbarism that has become one of the major philosophical and social facts of the last ten years at least. But we had better learn, and fast, that "civil liberties" isn't simply a liberal catchphrase but a foundation of our own domestic security. Yet protecting civil liberties—our own and those with whom we disagree—doesn't mean we become "civil libertarians," as that phrase is used by liberals. The barbarism that has become an almost accepted part of urban life in America came as a shock to us, for whom the neighborhood was not only a place to live but a way of life. Rape, mugging, burglary, arson: onward gallop the four horsemen that brought the new revelation of barbarism to the city.

We should demand nothing less than safety. If a politician can't deliver safety, let's dump him. And, let's acknowledge our own shortcomings. Too often in the past, we have been deceived and betrayed by our own kind as much as by the liberals and the intellectuals. There are too many Hagues and Kennys in our past for us to keep on being duped by those from our background who promise us everything, yet give us nothing but the crumbs from the table. In the old days we were duped by our own kind because they were very much like us in style and speech and custom. But in recent years we have been duped by a new kind of political con man. Midge Decter, writing in *Commentary*, said about their philosophy:

> (It) is the assertion of the right of those properly endowed—by education, upbringing, leisured high purpose, and, yes, by birth, if need be—to rule. The New Politics, even for the "kids" who find other names for it, is the assertion of the right to be ruled by attractive men, morally attractive, aesthetically attractive, in a morally and aesthetically attractive society. Both create the political ambience in which it is more suitable to speak the language of class: to speak of an individual man's "instincts," his "style," his "sympathy for," rather than to engage in a hard and clear examination of whose interests are being served by a given political impulse. And both create, though their adherents refuse or pretend not to know it, the vision of a political future which for a democracy cannot be a vision of openness, fluidity, but just the opposite. Theirs is the stuff from which Establishments are really made.
>
> The demand to be ruled in an attractive way is a reactionary demand—regardless of the radical rhetoric in which it may be couched. The alliance it bespeaks between the privileged and the *lumpen* and against the coarse-grained and sometimes brutal equalizing of the middle is nothing new to the history of Western politics—though the extent to which it has taken hold is new indeed to the history of 20th-century America . . .

This "demand to be ruled in an attractive way" brought with it a new class which exploited urban conservatives and for a few years they had their way. The New Exploiters are those who create costly, unworkable government programs and who milk every last tax dollar from the urban conservatives. The New Exploiters are much more crafty and shrewd than the robber baron capitalist exploiters of legend and infamy. The old-style exploiters flaunted their wealth and drove the downtrodden into rebellion on many fronts, particularly, of course, through the organization of unions.

But the New Exploiters are for the most part hidden and silent. Their exploitation is not so crass as to look like exploitation; it looks like do-goodism. But it exploits just the same. The liberal academics and intellectuals who have been adding programs by the dozens don't care who pays for those programs. In fact, our money isn't one of their chief concerns. Some, a few, don't even care if they get a lot of money themselves. What they want—and what they have gotten for years—is power, the power to shape the direction of the country through federal control. By the testimony of the liberals themselves, their efforts to build a Great Society—so it will be great for them and their clients and sycophants—have failed and the failure has cost the urban conservative not only money but a loss of spiritual confidence in his country.

For the New Exploiters to tell us that it is the "corporations" who are exploiting us is *chutzpa* to the tenth power. It is precisely the New Exploiters, the political and intellectual and media élite, who are the equivalent of the robber barons. Their robbery is, of course, much more subtle and, naturally, in the best of taste, but it is robbery none the less. They have robbed this country, not merely of money, but of pride. For them now to demand that we dance to their old, wheezy tune is obscene.

In the past, the New Exploiters were allowed to get away with their experiments with our money because too often we tolerated politicians whom the New Exploiters could easily manipulate. Lyndon Johnson, from all accounts, was of two minds about the New Exploiters: the "Texas" part of his mind knew them to be the fanatics and phonies they were; the "Presidential" part of him trembled with delight when they said nice things about his (their) programs. When he was no longer of use, they walked over—and out on—him.

We can't afford to make the same mistakes again. If there is any truth to be learned from the past ten years, it is that liberals practicing liberalism, or "on duty" as William Buckley put it, cannot and do not share any common philosophical interest with us. And that is where the ballgame is won or lost. The philosophy of liberalism remains even if liberals come and go and change their tune. They had their chance and they blew it.

What is it we want? We want a strong country, the strongest in the world because we aren't going to rely on mutual manifestations of good will to keep this country free. It is a tough world. The liberals think anyone who says that is practicing a false, twisted masculinity. So be it. We have been called everything else by the liberals; we might as well be called sexual psychopaths. But at the same time, let's demand that our nation be so strong that no nation or group of nations will ever dare attack us—or even *think* of attacking us. After we get that settled, then we can begin to work on whether or not we are loved.

We don't trust the Communists. We never will so long as they are Communists. We can't see why we should. There is nothing in the historical record or in the philosophy of Communism to suggest that anybody above the mental age of six should trust them. Not only that, we should positively *dislike* them. We can live with them and despise them at the same time. What they represent is everything this cruel century has told us about despotism. Everything evil the Nazis did, the Communists either did before them or to a greater degree, or both—the difference being that many of the commanders of the Nazi concentration camps have been brought to trial when found, while the ideological thugs responsible for the Communist slave labor camps are now in power and have been for years.

This doesn't mean we have to strike a pose as a nation. It just means we get our nation's mind set as to exactly what the world is all about.

At home we want: prosperity, safety and justice.

In our nation's relations with other countries we want: enough military strength to prevent war; a rational "America first" attitude avoiding the extremes of expansionist jingoism on one hand and isolation on the other; and a cool but correct attitude toward totalitarian dictatorships that have the potential to destroy our nation.

We believe this is a good country. We believe that our way of life, our values, our adherence to formal religion, to the family, to what Chesterton called the "decencies and charities of Christendom" have for too long been abused or ignored or threatened by left-liberalism. Left-liberalism is intellectually, morally, and spiritually bankrupt. We don't want it to be replaced by radicalism of the left or right. We want our kids to grow up knowing not only their prayers but their philosophy, our philosophy.

What is it that we want?

I'll tell you . . .

We want America.

Index